MAJESTIC MOLOKAI:

A Nature Lover's Guide

Magical evening clouds hover over the unusually serene sea and rugged palisades of Molokai's dramatic north shore.

By Angela Kay Kepler
& Cameron B. Kepler

MUTUAL PUBLISHING

The languid atmosphere of old Hawaii pervades
the rural stretches of Molokai's southern shore.

LCC# 91-067619
ISBN 0-935180-73-7

First Printing November 1992
123456789

Mutual Publishing
1127 11th Avenue
Honolulu, Hawaii 96816
Telephone (808) 732-1709
Fax (808) 734-4094

TABLE OF CONTENTS

ACKNOWLEDGEMENTS

In July 1966 we spent the first night of our honeymoon at the Molokai Seaside (now Pau Hana) Inn— in single beds! Our first thanks are to the unknown Molokai folks who spontaneously sang a heart-melting "Hawaiian Wedding Song" as we walked shyly into the lobby — how they knew we had just been married is still a mystery.

That was just a beginning. It has been a privilege to come to know this land and her people, and to help those dedicated to protecting her natural treasures, especially from 1977 to 1987. Thanks are due to several organizations who shared our exploration of its rugged hinterlands: U.S. Fish & Wildlife Service, Hawaii State Department of Land & Natural Resources (DLNR), The Nature Conservancy of Hawaii (TNCH), Molokai Ranch, Mauna Ala Hiking Club and several private landowners.

We will never forget those who shared dripping tents crawling with earthworms, precious morsels of food, droplets of water, nasty storms, and scorching sun; who fixed vehicles, checked our positions with radios, or who hiked with us. They include: Tim Burr, John Carothers, Rob Hansen, Alan Holt, John Kjaargard, Stephen Mountainspring, Ted Rodrigues, J. Michael Scott, and Kelvin Taketa. Our experiences with you are etched into our memories; because of you, we stand in awe of Molokai's grandeur.

Tom Hauptman (Pacific Helicopter Tours) and the late Ron Thrash (Royal Helicopters) at times risked their lives in powerful winds and enveloping clouds to drop us in remote areas. Mr. and Mrs. Richard Marks (Damien Molokai Tours), Randy Manaba and Jamie Manyer (DLNR), and Ed Misaki (TNCH) were generous with their time and energy. Special gratitude is extended to all photographers and organizations whose pictures enhance this book. Thank you also to Mr. and Mrs. Stumen, and Bruce and Nancy Woods for their hospitality; to Sue Nakamura for drafting the map; to Alan Holt, and Henry and Anwei Law for reviewing the manuscript; to Bonnie Fancher for secretarial assistance, and to Patti Provost for copy-editing.

A tidbit of wisdom from Kalaupapa.

PREFACE

DESPITE ITS DRAMATIC SCENERY and friendly people, Molokai (pronounced "moloh-kah-ee") has only recently been recognized for its positive "vibrations." Formerly named *pule-oo* ("powerful prayer"), the island's potent evil forces were feared throughout Hawaii. The unseen powers of its *kahuna* (priests/magicians), the inaccessibility of its rugged coastline, the scarcity of water in its inhabited areas, and its once-dreaded leper colony have all contributed to a history of isolation.

However, times have changed. Regular air service, scenic flights, rental cars (there is no public transportation), comfortable accommodations, and modern advances in the control of leprosy have made the island unconditionally accessible. Still, a sense of remoteness is manifest — it is as though Molokai's clock ticks more slowly than elsewhere.

This gem of an island has a split personality. One Molokai is hot, dry, almost slothful in its serenity. The visitor lingers to imbibe its quiet balmy air, tropical sunsets, and clear starry nights undimmed by city lights. The other Molokai is cool, wet, and brimming with drama and energy. This Molokai enthusiastically invites visitors to soak in gushing waterfalls, explore lush native forests, and marvel at its majesty. Geographically, this double personality corresponds roughly to an arid west and a verdant east.

Hawaii's fifth largest island, Molokai measures thirty-eight miles long by at the most ten miles wide. According to the *Molokai News*, the population is "6,500 friends." No point on the island is more than five miles from the ocean. Yet striking contrasts occur within this small area: the geography ranges from parched deserts to perpetually soaked bogs, from flat plains to the highest sea cliffs in the world.

Within the last fifteen years, exciting new phases in Molokai's historical evolution have been emerging — the discovery of bones from many hitherto unknown species of birds, the acquisition of Kalaupapa Peninsula by the National Park Service, and the active management of large tracts of Molokai's scenic and biological treasures by conservation agencies.

To help travelers make advance reservations, we have included some addresses. Phone numbers frequently change. For more detailed information, contact the Destination Molokai Association, P.O. Box 406, Kaunakakai, HI 96748; phones 808-567-6255 (Molokai), 808-941-0444 (Oahu) or toll-free 1-800-367-ISLE.

A word of advice: If you are rushed for time or seeking conventional entertainment, skip this island altogether. If you do choose Molokai, throw out your notions of "paradise" and be willing to rough it a bit. Listen to Molokai's ghostly tales, laugh with her children, feel the heart of her music, heed her secret whispers. Perhaps the "Friendly Isle" will captivate you, too, as it has us.

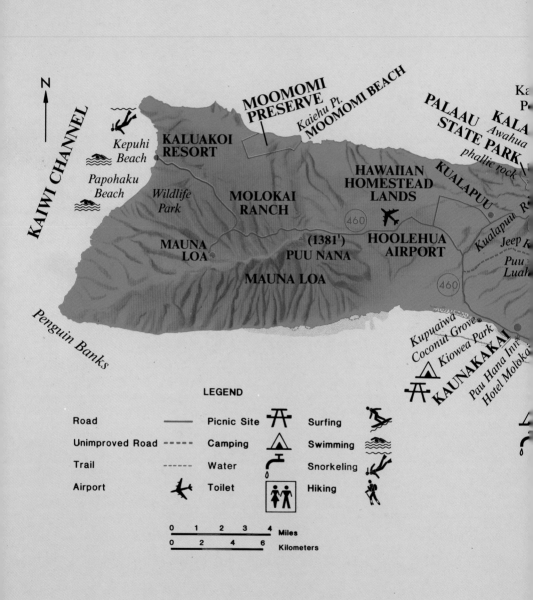

N

KAIWI CHANNEL

Kepuhi Beach

Papohaku Beach

Penguin Banks

KALUAKOI RESORT

Wildlife Park

MOLOKAI RANCH

MAUNA LOA

(1381')
PUU NANA

MAUNA LOA

MOOMOMI PRESERVE

Kaiehu Pt.
MOOMOMI BEACH

PALAAU STATE PARK

Awahua

phallic rock

Ka
P

KALA

KALA

HAWAIIAN HOMESTEAD LANDS

KUALAPUU

460

HOOLEHUA AIRPORT

460

Kualapuu R.

Jeep R

Puu Lual

Puu Lual

Kupuaiwa Coconut Grove

Kiowea Park

KAUNAKAKAI

Pau Hana Inn
Hotel Moloka

LEGEND

Road	——	Picnic Site	⛩	Surfing
Unimproved Road	-----	Camping	⛺	Swimming
Trail	-----	Water	🚰	Snorkeling
Airport	✈	Toilet	🚻	Hiking

```
0   1   2   3   4  Miles
0     2     4     6  Kilometers
```

6

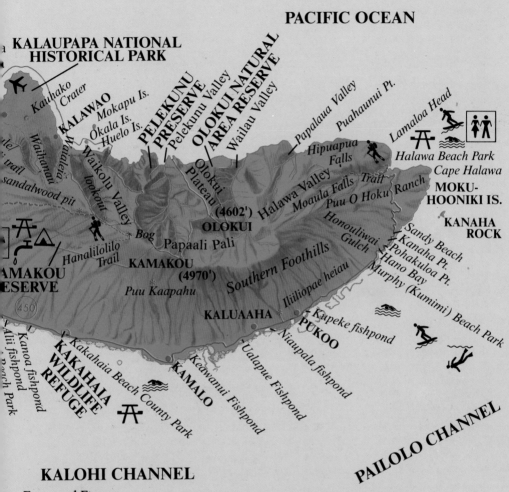

PACIFIC OCEAN

KALAUPAPA NATIONAL HISTORICAL PARK

Kauhako Crater

KALAWAO

Mokapu Is.
Okala Is.
Huelo Is.

PELEKUNU PRESERVE

Pelekunu Valley

OLOKUI NATURAL AREA RESERVE

Wailau Valley

Papalaua Valley

Puahaunui Pt.

Lamaloa Head

Waihanau

Waialeia

Waikolu Valley

lookout

sandalwood pit

Olokui Plateau

(4602')

OLOKUI

Hipuapua Falls

Halawa Valley

Moaula Falls Trail

Puu O Hoku Ranch

Halawa Beach Park

Cape Halawa

MOKU-HOONIKI IS.

KANAHA ROCK

Bog

Papaali Pali

Hanalilolilo Trail

KAMAKOU RESERVE

450

KAMAKOU

(4970')

Puu Kaapahu

Southern Foothills

Honouliwai Gulch

Sandy Beach

Kanaha Pt.

Pohakuloa Pt.

Hano Bay

Murphy (Kumimi) Beach Park

Iliiliopae heiau

KALUAAHA

Kupeke fishpond

PUKOO

Kanoa fishpond

Alii fishpond

each Park

KAKAHAIA WILDLIFE REFUGE

Kakahaia Beach County Park

KAMALO

Keawanui Fishpond

Niaupala fishpond

Ualapue Fishpond

KALOHI CHANNEL

PAILOLO CHANNEL

Facts and Figures

- The fifth largest island in Hawaii: 38 miles long by 10 miles wide at its widest point.
- Population 6,500 "friends", a high percentage of Hawaiian extraction.
- Highest sea-cliffs in the world: to 3,500 feet.
- Land area 260 square miles.
- The original home of hula dancing.
- Has a relatively high proportion of its land in natural preserves.
- The site of Hawaii's only Hansen's Disease (leprosy) settlement — now safe to visit.
- Excepting Niihau, the island where Hawaii's ancient spirit is strongest.

CHAPTER I WEST END

CLEAN, FROTHY WAVES pound against the expansive golden sands fronting Molokai's western shore. Each wave punctuates the evening silence with a thunderous roar. As the moments pass, one becomes progressively more attuned to the primordial elements of old Hawaii—land, sea, sky and the "spirit world"—all of which are particularly palpable on Molokai.

Even if your stay is brief, this island may touch you with its elusive spell. As the hot, glaring days melt, perhaps amid blazing skies, into balmy evenings, the west end unveils more subtle energies. A hazy luminescence in the aqueous distance—the only light visible except that of the low-slung resort—reminds us that bustling Honolulu is only twenty-six miles, and a generation or two, away. Timeless glimmerings seep into your awareness, nebulous perceptions of once-powerful thoughts and traditions.

The west end of Molokai covers almost half of the island's 260 square miles of land area. A single road (route 46) leads west twelve miles from Hoolehua Airport to the Kaluakoi region. This hot, scrubby, seemingly "empty" landscape, managed almost entirely by Molokai Ranch, is rich in island history. Its name is derived from *Kaluakoi* ("adze-pit"), the largest ancient *ahupuaa* (land-division) on Molokai. Within this 46,500 acres were several adze quarries, important resources for Hawaiians before metal became available.

The west end's extensive pastureland dates back to the vast land holdings of the famous King Kamehameha lineage. The entire 70,000 acres were sold in 1898 for $251,000, now the cost of a single condominium at Kaluakoi! Blocks of small houses and tilled holdings, primarily at Hoolehua, bespeak the success of the U.S. Congress in 1921 to allow people of at least fifty percent Hawaiian blood (currently twenty-five percent) to lease land for agriculture. This important Hawaiian Homes Commission Act was instituted at a time when the disenfranchised Hawaiian population had dwindled alarmingly as the result of 150 years of diseases and other Western influences.

The west end of Molokai is more than a vacation spot. In addition to having spacious beaches and enviable privacy, it was, and still is, of special religious significance to the Hawaiians. For centuries people lived here in harmony with the land and sea, blessed by a relative absence of war. Upon the gentle slopes of Mauna Loa (not to be confused with the grander Mauna Loa on the Island of Hawaii) the sacred hula originated and ancient seers communicated with the gods.

David Boynton

Ancient hula dancer

(right bottom, top left) On arrival at HOOLEHUA AIRPORT (elevation 450 feet), it becomes immediately apparent that Molokai is "laid back." Many of the residents have never left the islands.

(top) A warm matrix of community relations still exists on Molokai; everyone knows what everyone else is doing without having to explain. Try to imagine this AIRPORT SIGN anywhere else!

(left) Molokai, like Maui and Oahu, is a "volcanic doublet," formed from lavas flowing from two distinct volcanoes. This is obvious on Oahu and Maui, but less so on Molokai because the older volcano, MAUNA LOA, is little more than a rounded hill rising to only 1,381 feet at Puu Nana. It is noticeable, however, while driving toward the west end. Mauna Loa's "shield volcano" shape is seen here, looking across the Hoolehua plains from the east. Formerly sweet potatoes grew on its slopes, which receive more rainfall than the plains. Mauna Loa means

Kaluakoi Resort

"long mountain," a name that early Hawaiians also used for the earth's most massive (13,677-foot-high) volcano, located on the island of Hawaii. No native forests remain on this mountain or elsewhere on western Molokai. The former plantation town of Mauna Loa, still tiny, is gradually becoming revitalized.

Kapo sits in her darksome covert;
On the terrace at moo-he-laia
Stands the god-tree of Ku, on
Mauna Loa...

The original and most sacred school of *Hula*, founded by Kapo, the sister of Pele, (Hawaii's fire goddess), formerly crowned a secret knoll on Mauna Loa. In the above chant, the "god tree of Ku" was Hawaii's native ohia , and *moo-he-laia* was a place haunted by a divine nature spirit.

(above) This visual feast of unbounded space enthralls those who wander, mounted or on foot, along PAPOHAKU BEACH (pron. "pah-poh-ha-ku"), This glorious expanse of glittering coral sand, two miles in length and averaging 300 feet wide, is Molokai's largest beach and one of the longest in Hawaii. Its isolation could not protect it from military maneuvers in the 1940s though, nor from extensive sand mining operations from 1960-1975. Other beaches at the west end are off limits to visitors.

(right) The NORTHERN CARDINAL has spread to all the main islands since its introduction from North America in 1929. It is a common bird in the introduced forests and gardens of Molokai, and can often be seen along with the captive animals in Molokai's Wildlife Park.

(below) Molokai Ranch's WILDLIFE PARK, a 700-acre reserve lying near Papohaku Beach, offers visitors a guided safari. Its animals include ostrich, ibex, sable antelope, zebra, giraffe, and kudu from Africa, rhea from South America, and black buck from Asia. Several rare species were selected with the hopes of breeding them and selling surplus animals to zoos. The preserve, established in 1974, resembles an African savanna not only in its wildlife, but also in the abundant kiawe trees, close relatives of the flat-topped, thorny *Acacias* characteristic of East Africa.

Molokai Ranch

(left) The JAPANESE WHITE-EYE or *mejiro* (*Zosterops japonica*), seen here at its nest, was brought to Oahu from Japan in 1929, and has spread from sea level to the highest forests, becoming Hawaii's most abundant bird. Listen for its cheerful tinkling songs. These feisty little green birds even steal from sugar bowls and bread baskets at open-air eateries.

Robert Shallenberger

(below) Not a nocturnal recluse, the SHORT-EARED OWL (*Asio flammeus sandwicensis*) hunts rats, mice, small birds, and insects during the day. Known locally as *pueo*, this pale, round-winged owl is frequently seen soaring over Mauna Loa's pastures and scrubland.

Dann Espy

(above) A young MONGOOSE (*Herpestes auropunctatus*) attests to the reproductive success of a small Indian mammal. Introduced last century to control rats, these villains have acquired a more varied island diet. They have become a curse on chicken farms, and have nearly decimated ground-nesting birds. Coots, native duck-like birds, for example, can now breed safely only on floating nests over deep water.

Robert Shallenberger

(bottom) The KALUAKOI RESORT, Molokai's first and only luxury hotel/condominium complex, features elbow room as a standard attraction. Opened in 1977 — definitely off-the-beaten-track, though easily reached via rental car or shuttle service — it is more a private club than a resort. Its varied activities include golf, tennis, sport-fishing charters, a fifteen-kilometer jogging course, horseback riding, and instruction in hula, lei- and quilt-making, and coconut frond weaving. Simple pleasures such as strolling along secluded beaches, swimming, or picknicking are equally appealing. The associated condominiums, each with fully-equipped apartment units set amidst spacious landscaping, are Ke Nani Kai ("The Heavenly Sea") and Paniolo Hale ("Cowboy House").

(below) THE TYPICAL ROOM AT KALUAKOI is contained in an eight-unit cottage such as this. No crowded elevators or stuffy lobbies are to be found here. Second floor units have fifteen-foot ceilings, large fans, and unbounded views of the vivid blue Pacific.

Kaluakoi Resort

Kaluakoi Resort

(top) Ocean clarity is excellent here. Reef-building corals are primarily represented by *Pocillopora*, *Porites*, and *Montipora* species.

(center) The eighteen-hole, par 72 GOLF COURSE offers five beachside holes, artificial lakes, coconut palms, and a 200-foot-deep gulch slicing across the approach to one green. Fees are lower and tee times easier to schedule than on other islands. Landscaped, night-lighted tennis courts are also available.

James Maragos

Charlie Alding/Kaluakoi Resort

(below) Since the Kaluakoi region faces west and lies leeward of the tradewinds, stunning sunsets are common. Let their soothing, magical energies embrace your body, mind, and soul.

James Maragos

In Hawaii, the best beaches cluster around the older islands, where corals provide the raw material for golden sand. Molokai's west end encompasses a host of gorgeous beaches. KEPUHI BEACH, *(top, center, bottom)* a delight both in and out of the water, fronts the Kaluakoi Resort. Be careful — both Kepuhi and Papohaku (located just beyond the prominent headland at the southern end) are only safe on calm days. Heavy surf turns the persistent longshore current into a dangerous rip. Waves are occasionally outstanding for experienced surfers and bodysurfers *(below)* but hidden jagged rocks await the novice. Nearby is the starting point of the first successful swim from Molokai to Oahu, in 1961 — fifteen hours to Hanauma Bay.

James Maragos

(left) Brightening resorts and private gardens with brilliant masses of color — magenta, pink, yellow, red, and white — BOUGAINVILLEA (*Bougainvillea spp.*) is a year-round trademark of tropical splendor. Close scrutiny of this Brazilian native reveals that its visual appeal is derived not from petals, but from clusters of pigmented leaves, among which nestle tiny, white, tubular flowers.

(center) The RED HIBISCUS (*Hibiscus spp.*) and its captivating companions — lovely ladies, golden beaches, warm sunshine, luxury hotels, a relaxed lifestyle — have lured untold millions to Hawaii's Pacific-washed shores. Hawaii's official state flower since 1923, these versatile perennials come in a variety of colors and sizes representing both native and introduced species as well as man-induced hybrids. Though the plant blooms constantly, each flower lasts only a few hours before withering.

(right) Unrelated to true tulips, the AFRICAN TULIP TREE (*Spathodea campanulata*) hails from Africa. Continually budding off clusters of dazzling, frilly "tulips" in sunshine colors, these delightful ornamentals are today abundant in island landscaping.

James Hudnall

(top) HUMPBACK WHALES (*Megaptera novaeangliae*), migrants from Alaska, mate and calve in Hawaiian waters each winter. Although normally further offshore than on Maui, Molokai's leviathans occasionally cruise within sight of its southern and western beaches—between December and April.

Robert Abraham

(center) The waters off West Molokai teem with life. Penguin Banks, a shallow shelf, extends forty miles out to sea and harbors a rich fish fauna (but no penguins!). Only 17,000 years ago it was an emerged island. Diving equipment can be rented in Kaunakakai or through the resort. The ever-inquisitive TRUMPET-FISH (*Autostoma chinensis*) slowly prowls the reef, ready to scoop up unwary fish with an awesome inslurp of water. Farther out, divers risk their health and lives in waters over 300 feet deep to secure PINK AND BLACK CORALS for shaping into creative jewelry **(right)**.

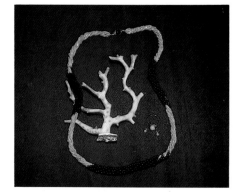

Robert Abraham

Snorkeling and scuba diving in crystalline waters is most rewarding, BUT *beware of strong currents and jagged rocks*. Gear can be rented at the resort.; guides are recommended. Pictured is a school of BLUE-LINED SNAPPER *(Lutjanus kasmira)*.

Fronting Kaluakoi, the island's largest resort, beautiful KEPUHI BEACH stretches north. Not long ago this was the exclusive domain of a ranch hand who tended cattle fences and water troughs in this formerly deserted corner of Molokai.

(*above*) Hawaii's shores have undergone radical changes, especially on the more populous islands. MOOMOMI BEACH (pron. "moh-oh-moh-mee") and adjacent lands are now protected by The Nature Conservancy of Hawaii. It owes its isolation to windy, rough weather and to Molokai itself, still relatively untroubled by crowds. Recently acquired by The Nature Conservancy, Moomomi houses biological, geological, archaeological, and palaeontological treasures, collectively unequalled in the state. It is also one of the few beaches where native Hawaiians may swim, fish, and collect *opihi* (limpets), seaweeds, and salt as their ancestors did.

(**right**) The weather on Molokai's north coast is renowned for its strong winds and stormy seas. For over a million years these natural erosive forces have sculpted THE COASTLINE, producing precipitous sea-cliffs, rocky headlands, crescentic coves, caves, and islets.

(right) Planes fly along Molokai's Moomomi Beach and its associated finger-like SAND DUNES, seen creeping across the island, revealing the inexorable path of Hawaii's tradewinds. Moomomi marks the low point between Molokai's two volcanoes. As winds funnel between the mountains, sands blow inland creating drifts that extend up to four miles. The Hawaiians named this area Keonelele, the "flying sands." At this point of the flight, your stomach may also be "flying"; landing at Molokai's airport is always bumpy!

The dunes are actually museums of subfossil bird bones. Since the early 1970s they have yielded such a startling array of now-extinct birds — eagles, owls, flightless ibises and geese, crows, and small forest birds — that biologists have been forced to re-think island evolution. These exciting finds have spawned the discovery of further fossils from dunes and lava tubes on other islands, almost doubling the number of bird species known previously. To date, almost fifty new species have been identified by specialists Storrs Olsen and Helen James of the Smithsonian Institution, Washington, D.C.

(bottom) Moomomi's remarkable SUBFOSSILS, dating back several thousand years, include many newly recognized species as well as some known only from 19th century museum collections. This artistic portrayal of flightless geese is by H. Douglas Pratt.

Douglas Pratt

(left) Moomomi's dunes of yesteryear are the LITHIFIED CLIFFS of Kaiehu Point today. Heat, pressure, salt, and the parching sun have cemented the sand into tough, calcified strata *(bottom left)*. Flanking the western edge of Moomomi Beach, these cliffs formerly sheltered resident Hawaiians from wind and sun: charcoal, crab claws, limpets, and adze fragments can still be found here.

(center) Early Hawaiians favored the extended Moomomi area for fishing, fish-drying, and gathering a dense, flinty basalt prized for making adzes. (Prior to 1778 Hawaiians had no metal.) RAW SALT, also a precious commodity, was scraped from shallow rocky hollows above the high tide line. Rich in iodine and trace elements, it is still esteemed.

(bottom right) WEST OF KALAUPAPA the cliffs decrease in height, tapering to sea level at Moomomi Beach.

(top & center) Like miniature woolly silverswords, the silvery rosettes of the rare ENA ENA (*Gnaphalium sandwicensium molokaiense*) stipple Moomomi's hardened sands. In order to survive the dry winds and brazen heat, this "beach daisy" has evolved special features to prevent desiccation. Thick layers of white-woolly hairs on its leaves trap air, reflecting away the sun's radiation in a manner similar to a mirror.

(bottom) Moomomi's coastal strand, though only a vestige of its original glory, still harbors many components of a major ecosystem. Windswept, stunted plants, both common and rare, struggle to withstand competition from introduced weeds and the ravages of feral deer. To date, five endangered species cling to life in this harsh environment, so dry it has been dubbed "The Desert Strip." Clinging tenaciously to survival, a few prostrate branches of the endangered OHAI (*Sesbania tomentosa*) dot the arid beach grasses. The people of old regarded this as a "royal" plant because of its reddish, pea-like flowers, which they fashioned into leis: red symbolized royalty, and that color in anything—a red feathered bird, red flower, red sailor's handkerchief — was revered. *Ohai* is so rare in Hawaii that virtually every individual plant is known, mapped, and protected.

23

(below) Moomomi fossils reveal that SEABIRDS AND GREEN TURTLES *(Chelonia mydas)* formerly nested here. Management of this newly-acquired 900-acre preserve includes safeguarding potential breeding sites for these special animals, as well as protecting its unique coastal vegetation, buried fossils, and stratified middens. Green turtles, *(Chelonia mydas)* are already emerging from the sea, and Laysan Albatrosses, *Diomedea immutabilis* **(right)**, with growing populations in the Northwestern Hawaiian Islands, may be enticed to breed here. Through enlightened management and responsible islanders, traces of former glory might soon grace these windswept dunes. Federal law prohibits the taking of sea turtles or seabird eggs.

Kilauea National Wildlife Refuge

(above) The GREAT FRIGATEBIRD (*Fregata minor*) is still known by its traditional name, *iwa*. This handsome seabird, which spirals effortlessly to great heights, features in folklore throughout the Pacific. In ancient times the *iwa* represented a thief, as it habitually chases other birds and forces them to regurgitate freshly caught prey in mid-air.

> *I shall find my songs in a small man's life.*
> *Behold them soaring!*
> *Very low on earth are the frigatebirds hatched,*
> *Yet they soar as high as the sun.*

> — *Return to the Islands*
> by Arthur Grimble (1957)

CHAPTER II SOUTH SHORE

THE LEEWARD SHORE is Molokai's most hospitable area and the easiest to explore. There is only one two-laned road, the Kamehameha Highway (Route 450), in fine condition for about twenty miles. The countryside, dotted with shoreline picnic spots and picturesque churches, is reminiscent of pre-Statehood (1959) Hawaii. This narrow lowland belt lies in the rain shadow of Molokai's mountains and is protected on its seaward side by a fringing reef as well as by the island of Lanai, nine miles distant. It basks in almost perpetual sunshine; average temperatures range from around 70°F in winter to 78°F in summer, and rainfall is a mere fourteen inches each year.

The gentle topography of Molokai's coastal plain allows easy movement from east to west. Early Hawaiians even built a trail along its entire length. The area harbors scant European history, however, as ship captains had difficulty finding anchorages. Now, as in times past, the bulk of Molokai's population clusters along this shoreline in a narrow band less than a mile wide.

Seven miles from the airport, Kaunakakai is the hub of island activity: the place to shop, eat, "talk story," and "fill 'er up" (gas stations are rare on the island).

Life in these parts is geared to the outdoors — hunting, fishing, picnicking, and partying. Many islanders resist changes that interfere with their chosen lifestyles. A typical weekend, for example, might involve camping at the beach, fishing, drying and mending nets, sharing barbecued fish, *poi* (cooked, fermented taro), beer and music with relatives and friends.

For sightseeing, casual clothes, comfortable shoes and sunglasses are recommended. Wave, and people will return your goodwill. A few families dotted along the south shore and east end (Chapter III) offer do-it-yourself or bed-and-breakfast accommodations in cozy country cottages. Beaches are shallow, rubbly, and muddy, but do not despair — some delightful sandy coves lie further east. In no other part of Hawaii does one encounter such a gentle sea, such an unruffled, langorous climate.

(*opposite*) Beach morning glory or POHUEHUE (*Ipomoea brasiliensis*), with mauve funnel-shaped flowers and leaves resembling goats' feet, is still a common beach plant in Hawaii. Native Hawaiians traditionally beat the ocean with *pohuehue* runners to induce the surf to rise, and used its sap to coerce the flow of mothers' milk.

(right) Coconuts frame THE WHARF, Kaunakakai's plain but picturesque "harbor," simply a dredged channel in the offshore reef. The original pier, begun in 1898, utilized coconut trunk pilings and all the stones from Puupapai, a large sacred *heiau* (temple). The building of the "modern" pier in 1934 required no such desecration. To find it, turn *makai* (toward the ocean) at Molokai's busiest intersection — a likely spot for the island's first traffic light. In case you blink and miss it, Rawlins Chevron on Route 45 marks the turn. Prearranged scenic and whale-watching cruises, as well as deep-sea sportfishing charters which troll for marlin, tuna, and *mahimahi*, all leave from here.

Some visitors complain that Kaunakakai is hard to pronounce. Phonetically "cow-na-kah-ky," it is actually a shortened form of "Kaunakahakai" meaning "beach landing." Molokai's major town, with over 3,000 inhabitants, occupies a former canoe landing site and beach reserved for royalty. It is still an anchorage, not only for Oahu's barges, but for fishermen, who have usurped the ancient royal prerogatives in building their huts here. Tumbledown SHANTIES **(center)**, adorned with dinghies fastened to insubstantial poles, line the shore west of the harbor road.

(bottom) Cute ISLAND *KEIKI* (children) visit the supermarket on shopping day.

(above) Every island in Hawaii has an official flower and color: Molokai is represented by the Polynesian-introduced *kukui* leaf and flower in green and white. During special celebrations like May Day and Kamehameha Day, PAU RIDERS (pron. "pa-oo" as in "too") and their horses deck out in intricate leafy leis, shiny *kukui* nut necklaces, and green satin gowns fashioned like traditional *pau* (ladies' long skirts).

(top) Several RESTAURANTS in Kaunakakai offer pleasant alternatives to hotel dining. Hop Inn occupies a western-style building that, along with its tin veranda and coconuts, is the essence of out-of-the-way South Seas town architecture. Close by, Oviedo's Lunch Counter and Rabang's Restaurant offer Filipino dishes. Across the street the Midnite Inn recalls former days: before commercial interisland flights, steamers bound for Oahu left Kaunakakai at midnight; the Inn stayed open to serve fresh fish and saimin (noodle soup with vegetables). Back in those days, passengers trundled into town via mule-drawn railcars. If you are travelling anywhere on Molokai, pick up food and drinks in town: country stores are few.

(center) An aerial view of Kaunakakai.

Simple serenity along the shores near Kaunakakai.

Molokai's famous KUPUAIWA COCO-
NUT GROVE adorns the coast about
one mile west of Kaunakakai. Almost
a century ago approximately 1,000
trees were planted by King
Kamehameha V on this ten-acre site.
"Kupuaiwa" was the King's nickname.
Today, the tall, slender "feather
duster" palms, visible from afar, are
cultural heirlooms. Although the Hawaiian people were less dependent on
coconuts than their South Seas neigh-
bors, this grove adds a Polynesian
mood to an island already brimming
with Pacific qualities. (Of more recent
vintage is the military "pillbox" in
foreground, set during World War II
to repel a Japanese invasion that
never materialized.) Coconuts may
fall, with fatal consequences, upon the
unwary *(right)*. Unlike elsewhere in
Hawaii, these trees are never trimmed
of their life-giving nuts. To Polynesians, coconut palms represent Life
itself; some rural families still plant a
coconut for each newborn child.

Adjacent to the grove is Kiowea
Park, a picturesque picnic and camping area with restrooms.

Landscaping around Kaunakakai is a reflection of the flowering and fruiting trees and shrubs that have been popular in Hawaii for a century or more. As in old Hawaii, and other cultures without a "throw-away economy," few fruits are wasted — the bounty is always shared.

(left) WILD or CHINESE MANGO (*Mangifera indica*), an old-fashioned variety with slightly stringy fruit, is common. Its yellowish fruits cook up into an excellent chutney.

(opposite, right) Originally from the South Pacific, the many varieties of colorful CROTONS (*Codiaeum variegatum*) thrive best in sunny weather.

(opposite, left) PINK TECOMA (*Tabebuia pentaphylla*), with its crinkly, petunia-like blossoms, originated in tropical America. It flowers year-round, particularly during spring and summer.

The scarlet ROYAL POINCIANA (*Delonix regia*), perhaps Hawaii's most spectacular ornamental *(opposite, top)*, brightens roadsides and gardens all along the south shore from March to October. This elegantly spreading tree, native to Madagascar, was brought to Hawaii in 1855.

White plumeria

Robert Abraham

(above) Proud of their heritage, Polynesians strike up tunes in the heart of Kaunakakai during the 1986 ALOHA WEEK PARADE (October). Behind the musicians lies Kanemitsu's famous bakery, over seventy years old, from which the majority of Molokai's baked goods originate. Don't be surprised to see pastry boxes being carried at the airport — it is a tradition to give these treats when visiting friends and relatives off-island. Listen for the local lingo, pidgin English, when you visit Kaunakakai... but don't try to imitate it.

(opposite page) Molokai folks, like all Hawaiians, love flowers. Celebrations, however trivial, provide excuses to make LEI. This complex one is woven in *haku*-style, where flowers and foliage are woven onto thin strips of dried banana trunk.

David Boynton

AGRICULTURE

For a century prior to the 1980s, Molokai was dependent upon cattle and pineapples for its economy. Today, with cattle ranching diminished because of bovine TB, and pineapple-growing virtually absent, the island is diversifying its economic base. Molokai's new agriculture is centered in the Hawaiian Homestead Lands near Kualapuu, Kalae and Kaunakakai, dispersed over small farms rather than in the former large agribusiness plantations.

Today Molokai's potentially productive areas are very arid, essentially lacking underground water. A large, rubber-lined aquifer in Kualapuu, fed by enormous quantities of water piped through the mountains from the north shore, supports limited agriculture. Water shortage is the major reason for the relative lack of development on this island.

Current crops include SHEEP *(bottom)* from New Zealand and Niihau, ONIONS *(opposite, bottom)*, of which many are marketed as "Maui onions," COFFEE *(below)*, and PLUMERIAS *(opposite, top)*. Enough plumeria blossoms for 600 leis — about 35,000 — are whisked off to Honolulu daily.

Two small hotels with neo-
Polynesian architecture, and two
resort condos are situated in, or close
to, Kaunakakai.

HOTEL MOLOKAI, an unpretentious,
yet comfortable, family-style hotel,
exudes a pleasant island charm similar to the Pau Hana Inn but different
from almost anywhere else in Hawaii.
With simple, airy comfort (each
room has a big fan), it is the place to
sit back and let the langorous climate, easy pace, tasty food, and island friendliness demonstrate the
pleasures of old Hawaii.

These two-story, high-roofed cottages are pleasantly landscaped with
coconut palms, bananas, and plumeria. Polynesian touches — private
lanai (porches) with big swings, cane
furniture, carved posts, and an open-
air restaurant overlooking the gentle
shoreline with distant views of Maui
— enhance the old-fashioned,
outdoorsy atmosphere. There is also
an oceanside swimming pool.

(*above*) Hawaiian music is performed
by KIMO PALAKA with a modest
gentleness typical of Molokai.

(top) The PAU HANA INN, Molokai's oldest hotel, provides charming shoreline cottages and a swimming pool. Representing an era long vanished on the other islands of Hawaii, this delightful guesthouse caters to locals as well as visitors. Pronounced "pow hah-nah," its name means "work's done," a common expression in Hawaii.

(center) A magnificent old Chinese banyan (*Ficus microcarpa*), gracing the ocean's edge by the Pau Hana Bar, provides an elegant, sylvan ceiling for dining and entertainment at the BANYAN TERRACE. Imagine its shadowed foliage etched against the starry firmament under a luminous moon casting pearly reflections upon quiescent waters.

(below) Step from your Pau Hana cottage at dawn for a glimpse of Molokai's south coast in a moment of magical stillness.

From Molokai's arid mid-elevation slopes, the south coastal plain appears as a narrow oasis of green framed by Kalohi Channel's sparkling waters and distant Lanai. In former times, innumerable streams and springs provided life-giving water, but these have mostly dried up as a result of deforestation. One "lake" remains — KAKAHAIA POND (pron. "kah-kah-ha-ee-ah"), a former inland fish pond used for raising fish and rice. Currently a sanctuary for endangered waterbirds, the fifteen-acre pond and thirty surrounding acres were purchased in 1976 by the U.S. Fish & Wildlife Service, becoming Molokai's first (and sole) National Wildlife Refuge.

(left) Kakahaia's GRASSY MARSHES support stilts, coots, herons, and migratory ducks. Active management includes fences and moats to deter dogs and mongooses, silt removal, and periodic flooding.

Visitors and residents alike find KAKAHAIA BEACH COUNTY PARK, six miles east of Kaunakakai, an inviting picnic spot. As the screens woven from coconut fronds *(right)* suggest, however, winds may arise, particularly after 10 a.m., providing welcome relief from the heat and a challenge for picknickers with paper plates and cups.

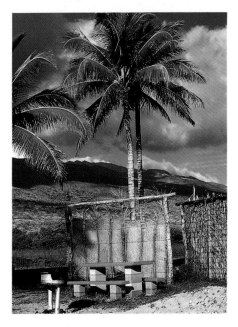

(right) CATTLE EGRETS (*Bubulcus ibis*) thrive in both wet marshes and dry pastures. About twenty inches high, they are very hardy. Insects are a major part of their diet. A few decades ago Cattle Egrets flew across the Atlantic Ocean from Africa to South America. They have subsequently colonized most of the world's warm areas, occupying a diversity of habitats.

(below) A BLACK-CROWNED NIGHT HERON or *aukuu* (*Nycticorax nycticorax*), a conspicuous, two-foot-tall gray waterbird (juveniles are brown-striped), rests between meals. Several night herons live at Kakahaia; others occupy shoreline or fish pond territories. Most conspicuous during low tide, they artfully stalk crabs or small fish in the murky shallows. Night herons were eagerly eaten by native Hawaiians, who chased them into swamps, pelting them with stones. All Hawaii's native birds are protected today.

Mike Boylan/Kilauea National Wildlife Refuge

Meyer Ueoka/Hawaii DLNR

Robert Shallenberger

A prominent white frontal shield, rising high upon its forehead, identifies this duck-like waterbird as an endangered HAWAIIAN COOT (*Fulica americana alai*). Unique to the islands, it is known locally as *alaekeokeo*. Coots are often superabundant in North America, but in Hawaii all waterbirds have suffered from the massive drainage of wetlands and the influxes of predators. Fortunately, growing numbers of coots, breeding year-round, attest to the increasingly effective management programs in Hawaii's fragmented wetlands.

Tim Sutterfield/Hawaii DLNR

A common denizen of Molokai's dry leeward forests and parks, the RED-CRESTED CARDINAL (*Paroaria coronata*) was introduced to Oahu in 1928. Originally from South America's eastern coast, this beautiful seed-eater spread throughout Oahu, colonized Molokai and Lanai, and is still expanding its range on the other islands. Both males and females are bedecked with a crimson bib and crest, pale belly, and slate-gray back. They are quite tame in outdoor restaurants, picnic grounds, and other public areas.

Howard Hunt

Perched jauntily in an octopus tree, the COMMON MYNAH (*Acridotheres tristis*) is a cocky immigrant that arrived from India in 1865 as part of a frantic effort to control insect pests in sugar fields. Starling-like, these ubiquitous brown birds are common throughout Hawaii's lowlands, favoring the haunts of man. Their white wing-patches are conspicuous during flight. They are often found roosting in noisy flocks.

Robert Shallenberger

Robert Shallenberger

Two widespread Asian immigrants, the medium-sized SPOTTED DOVE (*Streptopelia chinensis*, **left**); and smaller ZEBRA DOVE (*Geopelia striata*, **right**), inhabit semi-open, dry lowlands, where they forage for seeds on the ground or on roads. The former, whose island sojourn began in 1880, is less common than the latter which, though dating only from 1922, has adapted remarkably to its new home, actually becoming a pest in places. Diseases carried by birds such as these have contributed greatly to the demise of Hawaii's native birds.

Hawaii Dept. of Land & Natural Resources

(above) Perky and vociferous, GRAY FRANCOLINS (*Francolinus pondicherianus*) were introduced to the islands from India as game birds in 1958. They abound in Molokai's drier areas, and can be easily spotted during the first and last hours of day along Route 450 between Kaunakakai and Kamalo. Their piercing, repetitive morning call awakens the somnolent guest. They have a predilection for weed seeds and insects, and provide a tasty, though small, meal for the sportsman.

Robert Abraham

Hawaii, especially Molokai, is renowned for its fish ponds (*loko ia*), unique to Polynesia. Owned by Hawaiian royalty and built at their command, the ponds were created by enclosing shoal waters two to three feet deep within rock walls. These walls, averaging five feet deep and ten feet wide, represented monumental labor: Some exceeded 5,000 feet in length and occasional rocks weighed over 1,000 pounds. A matrix of sixty ponds, dating back about 1,000 years, extends along Molokai's south coast for approximately thirty miles. Stocked primarily with mullet and milkfish, the ponds provided a finny harvest all year, especially when ocean fish were off-limits. They were primarily used for storing and fattening fish rather than fish farming. Molokai's fish ponds rank among Hawaii's most enduring archaeological features. Two of them, at Keawanui and at Ualapue, are on the National Register of Historic Places. Keawanui, covering 54 1/2 acres, is enclosed by a 2,000-foot-long wall.

Fishing rods and lines can be rented cheaply in Kaunakakai. Camping is permitted beside the sixteen-acre Alii Fish Pond at Onealii Beach Park, four miles east of Kaunakakai. The State Department of Land and Natural Resources has detailed restrictions on bag limits, minimum sizes, and approved fishing methods.

(*top*) Most ponds are now abandoned but some, like KUPEKE FISH POND, are still alive. Unfortunately, Molokai's recent attempt to diversify agriculture has been unsuccessful in regard to aquaculture. Poor productivity of the fish ponds is due to excessive siltation from the badly eroded mountains, choking by introduced mangroves, and competition from introduced fish such as tilapia.

45

James Maragos / The Nature Conservancy

(top) Twilight at KUPEKE FISH POND: a clear, expansive sky imparts a soft glow to the low vegetation as gentle waves tumble on an offshore reef.

(center) The SUBMERGED REMAINS of an unnamed pond, recently discovered by aerial photography, arch from the seaward wall of Niaupala Pond. Sluice gates, long gone, allowed small fish to enter and prevented large ones from escaping. They were the inspiration for this tidbit of Hawaiian wisdom: "Open the fish pond's sluice gate and let the fish out." In other words, break away from bad habits and you'll have good friends.

(bottom) West of Kaunakakai, red mangroves *(Rhizophora mangle)* fill in ancient fish ponds, now saltwater marshes. Native to tropical America, red mangroves were introduced in 1902 by the American Sugar Company to stabilize Molokai's mudflats.

(left & below) Despite poor yields, local fishermen still derive much satisfaction from torch, net, and line fishing, as well as squidding in the shallows. Fish ponds were traditionally built along Hawaii's coasts where barrier reefs enclosed coastal lagoons: Molokai's south shore, Oahu's Pearl Harbor and Kaneohe Bay, and Maui's Hana Bay. Here low tide reveals a substantial FISH POND WALL.

(right) SUBDUED LIGHT imparts a satiny luster to the ocean, silhouetted by Kanoa Fish Pond's enclosing boulders. Bountiful catches from these ponds gave Molokai the reputation as "a land of plenty."

On Molokai's south coast, life for an ancient Hawaiian was not greatly different from his self-sufficient counterpart of today. His allotted *ahupuaa* (long-
triangular strip of lowland, foothill and upland environments) provided all
material necessities. Fish ponds provided protein; streams harbored shrimp
and freshwater shellfish as well as irrigating crops; and forests yielded wood
and medicines. Many contemporary residents pattern their lives similarly:
they fish in the same ponds and in the ocean beyond, grow taro and bananas,
and hunt in the mountains.

Molokai men still utilize centuries-old fishing techniques. (The average
Polynesian, even today, is much more attuned to Nature's ways than the average Westerner — unless a trained naturalist.) Night fishing, for example, is of
two types: "moonlight" and "dark night," involving fish who either follow the
moon's light or avoid it. Adherence to the "old ways" while selectively em-
bracing new ideas is a basic island philosophy. Their nets, for example, are nylon. Although no one knots them using hand-twisted natural fibers anymore,
most men still know how to mend, care for, and fish with them using time-
honored Polynesian techniques.

For an islander, VIVID SUNSETS are not only to be enjoyed esthetically —
they often herald a good night's fishing.

(above) Larger fish such as UHU (parrotfish, *Scarus spp.*), daytime foragers, haunt rocky points. Their blue-green colors (maroon in females) and parrot-like "beaks" provide easy identification. Today spearing is common, but formerly fishermen trapped *uhu* in woven baskets containing live decoys. *Uhu* is famous in folklore. One of its roles was that of a "tattletale," warning the fisherman of his wife's infidelity. If two *uhu* were seen rubbing noses, leaping out of the water, or adopting dubious postures... it was time to hurry home!

David Boynton

(above) AWEOWEO (*Priacanthus cruentatus*), whose bright red coloration, curious vertical mouth and huge eyes betray its nocturnal habits, is widespread in the world's tropical oceans. Its Hawaiian name means "glowing red." Long considered a delicacy in Hawaii, it grows to twelve inches and was formerly dried in great quantities. Periodically it appears in unexplainably prodigious numbers. As red was a sacred color in old Hawaii, it takes little imagination to clarify the old belief that such appearances signified the death of a high chief.

David Boynton

After work, weekends, holidays — Molokai men are always anxious to spend time on the rocks or at the beach catching a meal.

A typical shoreline along the south coast.

Robert Abraham

A circular nylon net, weighted around its circumference, poises in mid-air before pouncing on its submersed prey. Perhaps this THROWNET FISHERMAN will capture his favorite fish, the silver aholehole, as it flashes frenetically in the shallows.

David Boynton

A day's fishing bounty.

On a rare rainy day, RAINBOWS and clear gray skies highlight veteran monkey-pod trees amidst lowland pastures. In old Hawaii, as in many ancient cultures, the rainbow was an auspicious symbol from divine beings:

> *Hina* came down from heaven,*
> *Her way was by the rainbow...*
> — *Hawaiian chant*

*goddess of the moon and mother of Molokai

As the south shore blends into the east end, BEACHES becomes sandier and more swimmable.

(top) Most of Molokai is "make-do"; don't be alarmed to find yourself FORDING AN OVERFLOWING STREAM along the "highway."

(center) FISHING NETS, knotted in traditional Polynesian style and draped over wooden porches, lend a timeless quality to rural cottages.

FISHING AND CAMPING *(below)* and TENDING HORSES *(bottom)* are vital aspects of a typical Molokai lifestyle. When seaweed (*limu*) was more abundant, island women regularly collected it on such a beach, sorting different types to fill their hand-woven baskets. *Limu*, a rich source of vitamins and trace minerals, was a necessary supplement to the old-timer's basic diet of fish, poi and sweet potatoes.

Jacob Mau

"RODEOS" and equestrian meets, the two major events occurring in June and September, provide weekends of excitement to rural islanders.

Recently converted into a comfortable, well-signposted road, Route 450 traverses many miles of KIAWE FOREST (*Prosopis pallida*). This ubiquitous lowland tree, originally from Peru, shows remarkable environmental adaptation; the southern foothills are clothed in rolling mauve-gray expanses that appear to be dying, whereas the moist coastal belt is lush. Encounters with this spiny tree may include delicious *kiawe*-broiled fish, *kiawe* honey, a flat tire, or a piercing stab in your foot. Common in both built-up and rural dry coastlines, it sheds dead twigs armed with sharp spikes: be careful where you tread. Along this road, in 1792, where Kawela Gulch meets the sea, a bloody battle raged when King Kamehameha I invaded Molokai.

(left) The coastal plain broadens near KAMALO, four miles beyond Kakahaia, providing an expansive view of its idyllic ranch. Today's pastures, scattered dwellings, and a tiny jetty reveal traces of former habitation and agricultural bounty. Distant waterfalls, rarely seen close-up, plunge from Molokai's jagged, central backbone. KAMALO GULCH *(right)* rises grandly from the shoreline. The ridge to the right culminates in the island's summit, Kamakou (4,970 feet). Lava spewing from this volcanic dome 1.5 million years ago created East Molokai. Ekahanui Stables at Kamalo Ranch offers a variety of daily horseback rides in this area.

(above) Just past the tiny village of Kaluaaha lies OUR LADY OF SORROWS CHURCH (1874), the first Catholic church outside Kalaupapa's leper colony. Recently renovated, this picturesque, classic-style house of worship nestles among clustered palms. A life-size statue of its builder, Father Damien, stands in an adjacent pavilion.

Goats, deer and pigs (see Halawa Valley) are responsible for the extreme unhealthiness of most of Molokai's varied ecosystems. The island's domestic and agricultural water supplies, her fishing grounds, and intrinsic natural beauty must be preserved, not only for the economy and esthetics of future generations, but for Hawaii's present survival. Photos show denuded mountain slopes and the effects of siltation on the south coastal plain and offshore coral reefs (*opposite page*).

James Maragos / The Nature Conservancy

James Maragos / The Nature Conservancy

Denuded ridge in Kawela - Kamalo area.

James Maragos / The Nature Conservancy

SILT DELTA, Kamalo gulch. Scientists calculate that sediment in fish ponds in this area has accumulated at the astounding rate of one foot per year for one hundred years.

James Maragos

An underwater view of dead coral reefs, choked by siltation. This is typical of Molokai's entire south shore.

Parched and wasted, Molokai's south-facing slopes have supported a free-ranging herd of goats for over 200 years. These voracious nibblers, highly adapted to aridity, have decimated hundreds of square miles of dryland forest throughout Hawaii. Hawaii is not alone; governments around the globe are attempting to eliminate goats from island haunts. Pictured are PUU KAAPAHU *(top)* and KAWELA GULCH *(center)*, both formerly rich dryland forests containing precious sandalwood.

GOATS, introduced to the islands as a source of food by the great navigators of the 18th century, Cook, Vancouver, and La Pérouse, have unfortunately created more havoc than help. Goat-hunting is a year-round sport; information may be obtained from the Hawaii State Department of Land and Natural Resources on any island.

State and Federal agencies, and The Nature Conservancy are co-operating with local hunters to severely reduce the goat populations on Molokai. In Hawaii, goat-hunting has an innovative twist: the "Judas goat" technique. When numbers in any given area diminish greatly, a "leader goat" is selected to make life easier for the hunters and save helicopter money! A conspicuous goat (preferably pale for easy spotting) is caught and fitted with a radio collar which emits a continuous frequency for months. Goats are social animals, thus the lone goat's bleating and body scents soon results in a small group. Periodically the helicopter picks up the radio signal and zeroes in on them, zapping all but the leader, who proceeds anew to provide the "kiss of death" to more companions.

Hawaii Department of Natural Resources

58

U.S. Fish & Wildlife Service/Jim Jacobi

(below) Hawaii's fragile environments, which evolved in the absence of terrestrial mammals, are also unequipped to deal with the extremely destructive AXIS DEER (*Axis axis*). With their beautiful spots, they resemble grown-up "Bambis". Originally from India, axis deer were brought to Hawaii in 1868 as a gift to King Kamehameha V. Their shipper, ironically, was Dr. William Hillebrand, a noted botanist who was one of the few people who appreciated the inestimable uniqueness of Hawaii's native plants. Today, their progeny range widely, denuding semi-arid lowland flats and lush mountain forests, especially on Molokai and Lanai. With over ninety percent of does raising fawns annually, the rapid proliferation of deer needs curtailing. The deer-hunting season is in spring. Note the serious bark stripping in photo at left.

Hawaii Department of Natural Resources

ILIILIOPAE HEIAU

Molokai has always supported relatively small numbers of people. Her island-ers' strength was not warfare but religious power. Numerous *heiau* (temples, shrines, and refuges) and a plethora of tales relating to mythological creatures and eerie happenings, attest to its viability. Today the omens and blessings of authentic *kahuna* (priests) are still respected.

ILIILIOPAE HEIAU (pron. "eely-eely-o-pie hay-ow"), the largest and oldest structure on Molokai, belonged to the most sacred order of temples (*luakini heiau*) in Hawaii. This remnant "cathedral," as ancient as many a noble Euro-pean edifice, has recently been added to the National Register of Historic Places. Its original grass thatch and structural supports are gone, but the raised stony platform is largely intact. It lies in Mapulehu Valley, one-half mile in-land from Route 450. There is no sign, but a gate and trail close to mailbox 234 mark the spot. This is private land, so please respect the owner's rights. It is now possible to visit the *heiau* on a new tour, the Molokai Wagon Ride, of-fered as an "insider's" view of the countryside.

Iliiliopae was no ordinary "church"; its consecration required two weeks of high-powered ceremonies. Owned by ruling chiefs, it was a sanctum of intense prayer; an abode of universal deities and minor demigods; a site of chilling hu-man violence; and an altar for offerings of gratitude, appeasement, and ritual fire.

(*opposite*) The football-field-sized HEIAU PLATFORM is 286 feet long by 87 feet wide. Built in a single night, so tradition relates, by Hawaii's mythical *menehune* ("little folk"), its waveworn boulders were conveyed hand-to-hand across the precipitous central mountains from the north coast.

(*above*) STONE OFFERINGS wrapped in *ti* leaves (broad and shiny) may be found in a variety of locations on Molokai: by a waterfall, beside a trail, on a *heiau*. They symbolize prayers; please do not disturb.

(*right*) The sacred STONY TERRACES have survived for centuries. An adjacent mango grove, a shrine of shady greenery, is one of Hawaii's largest.

CHAPTER III EAST END

AFTER MILES OF ARID COUNTRYSIDE, the flourishing verdure of Molokai's east end is a welcome treat. Past Pukoo, Route 450 deteriorates progressively, but this inconvenience is amply compensated for by fresh breezes, curtains of luxuriant vines, and a tangible aura of remoteness.

The south shore's fringing reef and shallow lagoon-like waters, along with the last fish pond, give way to rocky coasts with pounding waves, inviting bays, and sandy coves. This region, wilder with each curve, has altered little in decades; changes are measured by feet of plant growth rather than by urban sprawl. Even the number of hotels (zero) has not changed. However, this "non-development" is not accidental. As you enjoy the rural scenery, pause a moment to respect those who tenaciously battle with developers in order to retain their preferred lifestyle.

After closely skirting the ocean the road narrows, climbing steadily up to rolling pasturelands. After reaching an elevation of 750 feet, it zigzags downward, tunneling in places through lush vegetation. Here you'll find many roadside edibles — papaya, guava, passionfruit, breadfruit, Java plum, mango, and coconut.

At the road's end, twenty-eight miles and more than one hour from Kaunakakai, is Halawa Valley. Tantalizing views of its twin waterfalls and curvaceous estuary can be glimpsed through the lush vegetation. Halawa's expansive, green-carpeted valley, encompassing 9,000 acres and bounded on three sides by steep, buttressed ridges, is one of Molokai's most rewarding destinations. Be sure to bring mosquito repellent, a raincoat, sunglasses, drinking water, food, and old clothes. If you hike upriver, be prepared for discomfort. The trek, though relatively flat, involves crossing a whirling stream that may be waist-deep, and trudging through plenty of mud.

(*opposite*) Approaching Halawa Valley, the 500-foot Hipuapua Falls spills down a rugged mountainside. Luxurious coolness pervades the air — how different from the parched glare of the lowlands a few miles back! It may be reached by careful boulder — hopping from Moaula Falls.

(top) CURTAINS OF VINES — morning glories and passionfruit — smother vegetation, power lines, and roadside fences. We are now moving out of a rain shadow area; the east end receives bountiful moisture from the northeast tradewinds.

(center) Wild PAPAYA TREES dot the roadside as it approaches Halawa Valley. Sample their sweet juiciness if you can reach them, but be careful of steep cliffs and respect fences.

(below) Looking westward as the road begins to climb, you'll appreciate popular MURPHY BEACH PARK (Kumimi).

(top) At POHAKULOA POINT ("long rock point"), the road borders a rough shoreline. In the absence of a protective barrier reef, waves crash unrelentingly upon this craggy, basaltic coast. Although this is Molokai's best surfing spot and a popular rock-fishing point, it remains relatively undisturbed. Native strand plants creep over the rubbly rocks.

(center & below) Pulverized coral reefs, washed ashore into intimate crescent beaches, greet the traveler. SANDY BEACH is choice among this four-mile string of pretty coves. Featuring pearl-white sand, it is partly protected by a reef, affording fine swimming and snorkeling. Watch for a rip current on the right!

(right) Picturesque bays abound; rolling, rugged scenery greets you as you wind around the shoreline. Pictured is HANO BAY, a seaward inlet of Honouliwai Gulch ("bay of dark blue waters").

(center) The undulating, 14,000-acre ranchlands of PUU O HOKU RANCH ("hill of stars") surround you as you approach Halawa Valley. The broad expanse of countryside *makai* (toward the ocean) and *mauka* (toward the mountains) is devoid of houses for miles.

(below) HORSEBACK RIDING, for both novice and experienced riders, may be arranged through Kaluakoi Resort.

Robert Abraham

MOKU-HOONIKI ISLAND

Mounting Molokai's eastern slopes, the road provides increasing panoramas across Pailolo Channel to Maui, nine miles away. Punctuating the strait is MOKU-HOONIKI (pron. "moh-ku hoe-oh-nee-kee"), whose Hawaiian name, "lover's pinch island," invites conjecture. This prehistoric cinder cone exploded from the shallow waters in a shower of coral fragments and lava. Subsequent pounding by the sea has split it, creating the rugged cliffs and the swirling currents we see today.

(top) Moku-Hooniki's DARK, CRUMBLY CLIFFS, dominating a distant view of Maui, provide a haven for several species of coastal plants and seabirds which can no longer survive on Molokai. Moku-Hooniki is now a Hawaii State Seabird Sanctuary, one of a handful of islets where written permission is required for landing.

(center) Hawaii is not all sunshine and clear skies — this photo was snapped on a drippy, but still warm, day.

Dawn's first light bathes KANAHA ROCK, the smaller of Moku-Hooniki's two fragments, in golden effulgence. Molokai lies beyond.

The WANDERING TATTLER, or ULILI, may be difficult to spot as it forages amongst the dark boulders of Hawaii's rocky shores. Watch for it along Molokai's eastern shore.

(center) WEDGE-TAILED SHEARWA-TERS (*Puffinus pacificus*), Hawaii's most common seabirds, have constructed nearly 1,400 earthen burrows on this pair of islands. In July their eggs hatch in an enlarged chamber at the burrow's end, where CHICKS *(above)* remain hidden for three months before emerging at night to venture into a far more dangerous world, the open sea. Known as *uau kani* (noisy petrels), they were once caught in great numbers as they flew back to their islands after fishing all day. Hawaiians lit smoky fires to bewilder the birds, then pounced on them with scoop nets. Wedge-tailed Shearwaters can be seen on shore cruises or fishing trips, especially around dawn and dusk.

(left) FALSE JADE PLANT (*Scaevola coriacea*) is extremely rare. Listed as endangered, it is now restricted to four tiny populations in the entire State of Hawaii, two of which are on offshore islands. On Maui they can be seen at the Kahului Zoo and along the Wailea Point beachwalk.

As your car zigzags down yet another ridge, Halawa Valley's SCENIC ES-
TUARY (above) suddenly unfolds its grandeur. Arising from a curvaceous,
bouldery strand (Halawa means "curved"), the mighty 1,500-foot cliffs of
Lamaloa Head signal the eastern terminus of Molokai's impassable north
coast. Around the corner you will see a wilderness of virtually impenetrable
vegetation and a few 3,500-foot-high waterfalls.

Halawa, one of the four precipitous, amphitheater-shaped valleys on the
island, is reachable by car. Despite its private ownership, you can picnic by its
churning waters, hike its dark inner recesses, become drenched in its frequent
downpours, delight in its tropical exuberance, sample its wild fruits, and swim
in its cool mountain pools.

Despite its isolation, Halawa housed some of the earliest native settle-
ments in the islands (A.D. 650). Its archaeology, chronicled by fishing imple-
ments, middens, *heiau*, and vestiges of huts, is well documented. Even as late
as 1836, 500 people lived here, nourished primarily by taro, fish, and shellfish.
After 1957, when a disastrous tsunami (tidal wave) struck, only a few
remained.

Sparkling sunshine after a downpour highlights HIPUAPUA FALLS (pron. "hee-poo-ah-poo-ah"), which plummets into the valley amidst canopies of monkeypod, *kukui*, and Java plum trees.

(top) Once in the valley, Route 450 forks; the rutted left spur leads you UP-VALLEY. The right spur leads to Halawa Beach Park, a spacious grassy area equipped with restrooms, pavilion, and barbecue grills. There is no potable water and camping is not permitted. Imbibe the salty air, stroll along the bouldery estuary, and watch the swirling ocean, on whose waves royalty surfed. There is a strong rip current here: do not swim anywhere if the stream is high.

A boat trip is offered (May to September) from Halawa estuary along Molokai's dramatic north shore to Kalaupapa Peninsula. (Contact Hokupaa Ocean Adventures).

(below) A popular hike past walled taro terraces and ANCIENT HOUSE FOUNDATIONS, *(bottom)*, is an excellent introduction to Hawaii's windward lowlands. Splendid views of the VALLEY HEADWALLS *(center)* vie with lush greenery for one's attention. To locate the trailhead, turn left at the road fork. Park soon, as there is no turnaround at the end. The four-mile, three-hour (round trip) trail is marked, but its lower portion has long been in a state of disrepair, and a locked gate prevents hikers from crossing the river via the bridge. Follow the muddy track to the river and prepare to get soaked. Do not attempt to cross if the stream is raging. Soon the indistinct trail from the river connects with a wide, muddy horse trail. (Note the water pipe, otherwise your return trip will be two miles longer and you'll end up at the stables by the ocean.)

Guided horse rides are also available through Halawa Valley Horse Rides.

(top) Molokai's official flower, with leaf and nut, is the KUKUI (*Aleurites moluccana*), easily recognized by its maple-like leaves and silvery foliage. Its oily nuts, similar to walnuts, when strung like a shish kebab, provided the primary source of lighting known to Polynesians, hence its alternate name, candlenut. Throughout Hawaii, certain *kukui* groves were considered sacred. Kalanikaula, en route to Halawa, is such a grove. It was so filled with *mana* (spiritual power) that one respected source considers it "the second most sacred spot to the Hawaiians." Today, standing serenely in a pasture, it is still *kapu* (forbidden).

(center) Abundant along dryish ridges is the CHRISTMAS BERRY (*Schinus terebinthifolius*). The clusters of small, inedible red berries — popular as hat decorations — brighten the roadside during fall and winter.

(bottom) YELLOW GINGER (*Hedychium flavescens*) in the wetter areas, possesses a honeysuckle-like sweet odor.

(top) The large, heart-shaped leaves of TARO (*Colocasia esculenta*) symbolize not only a staple food, but a deeply spiritual facet of Hawaii's culture as well. Taro was considered the progenitor of the human race; the embodiment of Kane, source of all life; and the source of fertility, prosperity, and long life. Until this century, Halawa, whose name also translates to "ample taro stems," was a major source of taro for both Molokai and Maui. The broad valley bottom was terraced intensively like rice fields. Commercial production continued until 1946 and 1957, when two searing tsunamis demolished the fields. JOE MOLLENA *(center)*, an Hawaiian-Filipino, now lives in Hoolehua. He was one of the last taro farmers, having left Halawa in 1959.

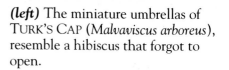

(bottom right) Another common hibiscus is HAU (*Hibiscus tiliaceus*), a Polynesian introduction which looks so much at home along shorelines that most people think that it is native. In the past, its cork-like inner bark was chopped into small pieces for fishing floats or shredded and twisted into twine.

(left) The miniature umbrellas of TURK'S CAP (*Malvaviscus arboreus*), resemble a hibiscus that forgot to open.

(top) PASSIONFRUIT: the shiny, "golden goose egg" fruits of this curiously named vine are plentiful near Iliiliopai *heiau* and further east, especially during fall. Of tropical American origin and now wild throughout Hawaii's moist lowlands, the fruit's name refers not to erotic pleasures but to the sufferings of Christ. Each portion of the plant sybolizes one aspect of the Crucifixion.

(center) GUAVA shrubs (*Psidium guajava*), bearing circular, lemon-sized, yellow fruits practically year-round, are conspicuous here. Sweet and juicy, with pink seedy pulp, each is packed with both vitamins C and A. Select large, knobby ones that are soft but not squishy. Fallen ones are often the sweetest, but may harbor worms. Guavas harbor pesky fruitflies, so *on no account consider smuggling any out of the state!*

(bottom left) BREADFRUIT, or 'ulu (*Artocarpus altilis*), lower right, with large, shiny, lobed leaves and head-sized fruits recalls "Mutiny on the Bounty."

(bottom right) PINK HIBISCUS (a Hibiscus hybrid) flares its five petals along the sunny roadsides.

(top) The impressive torrent of water spilling in a double chute, 250 feet over the escarpment at the end of Halawa Trail, is MOAULA FALLS (pronounced "mow-ah-oo-lah"). To appease the Hawaiian gods, throw a *ti* leaf into its spacious pool. If it floats, the undertow is weak and swimming is safe. However, observant visitors will note that water here is loaded with reddish silt, a result of heavy pig and deer damage upstream. Halawa's murky waters *(below)* are undrinkable, harboring animal-carried diseases that vary their effects from stomach upsets to death. The 1990s began an intensive effort to eliminate pigs using helicopters and state-of-the-art infrared and laser technology. This is carried out primarily by the State's Natural Area Reserve System, (NARS) and The Nature Conservancy (TNC).

This is also one of the rare spots in Hawaii which causes even skeptical people to suspect the existence of Hawaii's *moo* (legendary lizard women, pron. "mow-oh"), a mini-equivalent of the Loch Ness monster. Beware!

David Boynton

FERAL PIGS and deer have created havoc within native rain forests, seriously damaging water purity, creating health hazards to residents and visitors. On the Island of Hawaii *one-third* of the diggable area of rain forest is disturbed every year.

USFWS/Jim Jacobi

DEVASTATED FOREST above Halawa Valley. A tall rain forest once clothed this plateau. Now emaciated, this precious native ecosystem has been reduced to weeds and sickly treeferns, sunburnt survivors of a rich, shady forest. This subject is discussed further under "South Shore", p. 58.

CHAPTER IV NORTH SHORE

MAJESTIC, VIRIDESCENT ESCARPMENTS soaring to a dizzying 3,500 feet; immense valleys engulfed by enshrouding mists; ribbon waterfalls tumbling into crashing waves; craggy promontories and bold sea-stacks, such is Molokai's awesome north coast. The most dramatic juncture of land and sea in Hawaii, its only possible competitor is the spectacular Na Pali coast on Kauai.

Comparable to the breathtaking ice-carved fiords of Norway and New Zealand, this fourteen-mile stretch of sea cliffs has no higher counter-part. This is rugged wilderness with high wind and surf, frequent rain, difficult land access, and a tradition of isolation.

Powerful erosion by wind and water from every direction has, over a million years, carved a series of deep valleys that are easily identified from the air: from east to west — Halawa, Papalaua (shallow, but with a notable, 1,200-foot cascade), Wailau, Pelekunu, and Waikolu. The next prominent landmark is Kalaupapa Peninsula, site of Molokai's well-known leper colony.

On clear days the north coast sparkles with color — radiant blue skies, snowy whitecaps, crystalline waters, and a kaleidoscope of greens sweeping inland to Molokai's forest-clad backbone. The topmost cusp is Kamakou (4,970 feet), the island's highest peak and the remnant of a long-extinct volcano from which the massive lavas originally flowed to form East Molokai.

Commercial flights from Oahu to Maui regularly travel along this coast — weather permitting. Small planes fly lowest, affording closer views. A real treat, well worth the extra cost, is a scenic flight (helicopter or fixed wing) originating from either Maui or Molokai, which can be arranged through hotels or travel agencies on any island. See also page 74 for boat trips from Halawa Valley.

Overland access to Molokai's north coast is marginal: the south coast road (Route 450) terminates in Halawa, while the west rim of Waikolu Valley is accessible only to four-wheel drive vehicles.

The farsighted actions of several private and public agencies have combined to protect over 19,000 acres of this outstandingly scenic, biologi-cally diverse region, rich in Hawaiian history and worthy of national park status.

The highest seacliff in Hawaii, Olokui Plateau's IMPOSING RAMPARTS plunge 3,500 feet to the surging waves below. Kalaupapa Peninsula lies in the distance.

(top) Okala Island and Molokai's NORTH COAST glow in a magical summer sunset. Clouds, natural dominating features of the islands, are described in Hawaiian chants such as the following:

"Ye sombre clouds that rampant the sky;
Ye warm clouds and ye that gleam ruddy;
Ye clouds that guard heaven's border;
Ye clouds that mottle the heavenly vault;
Ye clouds that embark the horizon;
Ye cloud-piles aglow in the sunlight. ..."
— Anonymous

(below) High cliffs, succumbing to storms and the incessant battering of Pacific swells, often tumble into the implacable waves, forming shelves that project seaward. In time, these ephemeral landforms will themselves disappear, leaving unprotected cliffs to be etched anew. PUAHAUNUI POINT is the easternmost of five such tenuous "flatlands" between Kalaupapa and Cape Halawa. An Hawaiian family occupies a similar inholding close by, carrying out a subsistence lifestyle in possibly the remotest habitation in Hawaii.

The FOREST-CLAD SEA CLIFFS of Olokui Plateau frame a succession of spectacular profiles marching westward toward Kalaupapa's tongue-like peninsula,
long the home of lepers banned elsewhere in the islands. Once believed to be
a result of volcanic faulting, geologists now tell us that these impressive escarpments have been carved entirely by the formidable actions of wind,
waves, and water.

(top & right center) Like a giant thumb, 220-foot HUELO ISLAND points skyward, bearing on its slanted summit a rare forest of *lo'ulu* palms (*Pritchardia hillebrandii*). Although scattered palms occur on Hawaii's main islands such dense stands also occur only on remote Nihoa Island, north of Kauai. Elsewhere, rats and pigs have devoured their succulent seeds, resulting in poor reproduction. Prominent amongst the tufted grasses adjacent to the palms, the similarly rare, cabbage-like *pua ala* (*Brighamia rockii*), sporting five-inch-long flowers, thrives, inaccessible to any vertebrate except birds *(below)*.

(left) The imposing grandeur of Kalawao's towering cliffs highlights the 425-foot, tooth-shaped dome of OKALA ISLAND, where ancient Hawaiian youths, carrying huge pleated leaves of *lo'ulu* palms, reputedly climbed for the sheer thrill of parachuting harmlessly into the adjacent sea. Although protected as part of the Hawaii State Seabird Sanctuary, modern biologists have yet to scale its cliffs to determine which birds and plants remain here

RED-TAILED TROPICBIRD (*Phaethon rubricauda*): this sleek, graceful seabird breeds in small numbers high on the cliffs of Molokai, Lanai, and Kahoolawe. Soft, snow-white feathers from the *koa'e-ula,* as Hawaiians call them, were stitched into silken capes that were as luxurious as angora rabbit fur. The foot-long, crimson tails of these birds were also prized for *kahili,* the familiar royal insignia of bygone days, consisting of colorful cylinders covered with feathers from native birds. **(below)** A downy tropicbird chick.

Robert Shallenberger

(top) Pausing briefly, one of the authors ponders the slippery rocks and IMPOSING CLIFFS OF GRAY adjacent to Waikolu Valley, the first sight beheld by thousands of lepers as they struggled ashore to begin their exile in misery at Kalaupapa.

(below) To ancient Hawaiians, especially those dependent on fish for survival, the ever-changing MOODS OF WIND AND SEA were the subject of daily concern. Prayers such as this were frequently offered to the great gods: "*Awake! O mists driving inland. … The wild sea, the driving sea, the angry sea, the foreboding sea, the swelling sea, the rising sea, the swamping sea, the standing sea, and the boisterous sea. …*" Here, Okala and Mokapu, rugged seastacks, conspire with steep cliffs to fracture and funnel the incessant tradewinds, creating eddies and circular gusts that hurl the wavetops in every direction.

(left) Well-irrigated TARO PATCHES (*loi*, pron. "low-ee") once graced Waikolu's broad valley mouth. Today they still underlie a dense grassy carpet cropped by wild goats. Further inland, terraces, rock walls, ancient house sites, and medicinal plants silently recall the echoes of a thriving Hawaiian community that prospered here for more than 1,000 years, as well as the less fortunate lepers that followed, eking out a cruel survival far from helping hands.

(below) A "MODERN CABIN" under shadowy mango trees shelters Waikolu's twentieth-century inhabitants: hunters, workers fixing the water system for Kalaupapa, the odd wild pig lodging beneath the rickety floor, and a horde of smelly rats aided by the spoils of partly-eaten meals.

(below) Halfway up WAIKOLU'S WEST SIDEWALL, native trees frame a spectacular panorama. During stormy weather, each of the dozens of fluted indentations becomes engorged with roaring, 1,000-foot-high waterfalls, rushing toward the wind-whipped ocean.

Ribbon Falls in a vastness of green--the essence of interior Molokai.

WATERFALLS of ever-increasing grandeur grace the inland recesses of Waikolu ("three waters"). Just as the Eskimos developed numerous names for snow, so did the Hawaiians distinguish between different types of waterfalls. Our favorite word is the onomatopoeic *wailele* — "leaping water."

The Nature Conservancy · Hawaii

PELEKUNU (center of photo) and its eastern companion, WAILAU, are the great, amphitheater-headed valleys of Molokai. Their serpentine rivers and vein-like tributaries, surging under an annual deluge of 250 inches of rain, tear endlessly into the heart of the old volcano whose fiery lavas created East Molokai. With mighty erosive power they have completely isolated a major plateau, Olokui. Unscaleable bluffs, ensconcing the valleys from the outside world, also shield them from light. Near their headwalls, the sun penetrates the valley floors for only a few hours daily. Even the name Pelekunu means "smelly from lack of sunlight."

Swirling Mists from Pelekunu dissipate in the clear morning sun. The blue flagging tape is part of a scientific survey in 1980 which spearheaded protection of the valley and its neighboring cliffs and forests.

(right) One of Hawaii's prettiest coastal natives, NEHE (*Lipochaeta succulenta*) resembles a common landscaping plant, wedelia. Many of the twenty-six species of *nehe*, formerly common along shorelines, are aberrant in that they live within a stone's throw of the ocean yet their seeds cannot float! In old Hawaii, *nehe* leaves were occasionally brewed for tea.

(below) Pelekunu's FAST-FLOWING WATERS harbor a constellation of native aquatic denizens now rare elsewhere. All evolved into unique species from saltwater counterparts. Here freshwater limpets (*hihiwai*), goby fish (*'o'opu*), and shrimp (*'opae*) thrive in a wild river unhampered by dams. When dammed rivers occasionally dry up, all fresh-water animals are doomed, as they must return to the ocean to spawn. In this valley, three species of gobies, found at elevations as high as 1,300 feet, display a curious schooling behavior unknown elsewhere in Hawaii.

John Carothers

(top) The coastline between Pelekunu and Wailau ranges from modest ridges, talus benches, and bouldery beaches to the world's highest sea cliffs. In summer, a few locals with special ties to this dramatic shoreline, and small parties of experienced canoeists, camp here, if weather conditions are favorable. At Pelekunu, this TUMBLING SPRING entices two swimmers to drink of its clear waters.

(right) A less obvious relic of bygone days is the veritable cornucopia of Polynesian-introduced plants, transported in canoes from the Marquesan Islands as far back as 400 A.D. This TI (*Cordyline terminalis*) produces an immense root whose sweetish starch was eaten, fermented into "beer" and, during the nineteenth century, distilled into the dangerously alcoholic *okolehao*. Other established imports include taro, bananas, *noni*, *hau*, *kukui*, shampoo ginger and, rarely, lonely clumps of the narcotizing *awa*.

91

(right) Pelekunu, home to a thriving community of Hawaiians, was abandoned in 1931 after more than a millenium. They built taro terraces and STONE WALLS, such as this one on Puu Hoi ridge at 1,300 feet, to delineate boundaries and protect crops from marauding pigs.

(bottom right) The fingered fronds of LAUAE FERN, pron. "lah-why-ee," (*Phymatosorus scolopendria*) and frilly lichens unaffectingly portray Nature's artistry as they creep around a rotting log. Lauae, common on all Hawaii's , windward coasts, symbolizes romantic love, as in this nineteenth-century chant:
Rain ... clinging to the lauae ferns,
a fair sweetheart in the arms,
the sea sounding softly as if to say —
come back, we will be as one.

(center) Thick SHAMPOO GINGER (*Zingiber zerumbet*).

(bottom left) YELLOW GINGER (*Hedychium flavescens*) thrives on old taro terraces.

(top right) Fresh water from a
PERCHED SPRING flows from
Pelekunu's eastern sidewall. Aquifers
such as this one, trapped between
layers of dense lava, constantly re-
charge rivers and widen valleys as
they gnaw ever deeper into their par-
ent cliffs. Springs (*wai puna*) symbolized sweethearts in ancient Hawaiian
poetry.

(bottom right) Pelekunu Valley lies
embraced between the 2,500-foot
cliffs of Olokui (foreground),
Molokai's second highest peak, and
the awesome walls of Papaala Pali. A
filigreed network of silvery *kukui* trees
traces the routes of Pelekunu Stream
and its tributaries from the mountains to the sea.

(bottom left) Magically whisked to
the skyline of the previous photo, we
attain a new perspective. Here,
within Kamakou Preserve on a typical day, a MISTY, RAINBOW-CLAD
RAIN FOREST thrives, devoid of the
introduced plants that dominate the
valley below.

(right) All Hawaiian streams are
short; Pelekunu is no exception.
Three miles from the churning
ocean, its valley ends abruptly in a
2,800-foot palisade, mighty PAPAALA
PALI ("sun-burned cliff"). Its rocky
fortresses are here notched ever
deeper by Kawailena Stream's shadowed canyon.

(center) Catching skipjack tuna or
aku (Katsuwonus pelamis) off the
north coast.

(below) WAILAU VALLEY ("many
waters") slices deeply into Molokai,
helping to isolate Hawaii's preemi-
nent rain forest, Olokui Plateau. Inhabited by self-sufficient farmers till
about 1920, Wailau is now visited
only by occasional hunters, fishermen, and Sierra Club hikers. The latter are actively attempting to eliminate aggressive weeds. During the
1970s, Wailau experienced a period
of illegal marijuana harvests.

James Maragos

James Maragos

A RUGGED DARK VALLEY plunges 4,000 feet from Olokui Plateau to Pelekunu Valley floor. Its dizzying slopes, untrod by man or beast, are clothed in pristine forests of prehistoric grandeur.

Conservation agencies have long sought legal protection for Molokai's remarkable north shore and mountain uplands. The first major breakthrough came in 1981, with the establishment of Kamakou Preserve. Renewed interest focused on the area, and in 1986 a reserve was created on Olokui, while nearby Kalaupapa and its adjacent uplands were added to the National Park System. Isolated Pelekunu Valley was added to The Nature Conservancy's expanding preserve system in 1988, creating a 19,225-acre complex. The splendor and biological diversity of this entire area constitute one of the most dramatic spectacles in the world.

Pelekunu Preserve, a 5,749-acre wilderness recently protected, is also an integral part of Molokai's interior mountains. Its rugged terrain, rising from a windy, wave-pounded shore to a jagged, mist-enshrouded ridgeline, forms part of the island's geological heart. Within this expansive verdure dwell rare plants (including Molokai sandalwoods) and patchy populations of native birds that have acquired resistance to mosquito-borne diseases. Although normally confined in Hawaii to the upper limit of mosquitos (3,000- to 5,000-foot elevation), some native birds can survive down to 1,000 feet in Pelekunu. Photos show the heart of Pelekunu's intact native forest.

PELEKUNU VALLEY from Kolo Ridge.

John Carothers

(right) A thick sponge of MOSSES and ferns blankets the peaty soil, drapes over rocks, rotting logs, and gurgling streamlets, and even climbs high into the trees.

(bottom left) Almost constantly veiled in clouds, PELEKUNU'S BACKWALL supports a low cover of stunted shrubs and sedges. Dense forest, partly native, partly introduced, frames a view DOWN VALLEY from a sidewall at 1,000 feet elevation. *(bottom right)*. In order to protect the health and beauty of these remote forests and cliffs, more than 2,000 goats, 100 pigs and 75 deer were removed in less than 3 years (1988 — 1991).

CHAPTER V KALAUPAPA

KALAUPAPA: THE VERY NAME conjures up terrifying images of untouchable lepers disfigured by man's most dreaded curse. While nothing can undo the damage wrought by leprosy, modern medicine has removed the deadly fear of contagion.

Just as alien mammals and disease-carrying mosquitos drastically altered Hawaii's natural ecosystems, so too did Western diseases decimate its native people. Over millenia, Hawaii's plants, animals, and people had all naturally adapted to a variety of island habitats: plants lost their thorns, birds and insects lost their wings, geese lost their webs in their feet, and people lost the natural immunities to man's common maladies. When aggressive invaders, visible and invisible arrived, all were defenseless.

Leprosy, or *mai pake* (Chinese disease), the most frightening intruder, was first detected in the 1830s, but probably burgeoned with the first wave of Chinese immigrants twenty years later. Its microscopic bacteria, related to those that cause tuberculosis, spread like wildfire, selectively attacking Hawaiians with their poorly developed immune systems. More than ninety percent of its victims were Hawaiian or part-Hawaiian. They named it *mai hookaawale*, "the separating sickness."

By 1866 the epidemic had struck one out of every fifty people! Panic-stricken, King Kamehameha V decided to uproot the fisherfolk on Kalaupapa and designate their land as a leper colony in order to protect the healthy population. This action ushered in a poignant era of island history.

Those afflicted with the disease suddenly became outcasts. People from all walks of life, from babies to the aged, were trundled aboard boats in Honolulu and shipped to Molokai, never to return. Many families, through anguish and fear, not only said good-bye but completely severed all associations with their loved ones. Some even changed esteemed family names. Relatives lived in trepidation of "bounty hunters," spies for leprosy cases who could pocket a handsome reward for turning someone in. No words can describe the excruciating pain, the fear, the starvation, the base morality, and the bitter anguish of Kalaupapa in those early years. The only law was a natural "pecking order" wherein the strong ruled the weak. If ever there was a God-forsaken place, this was it.

In 1873, Father Damien, a Belgian and the first resident priest, arrived at lawless Kalaupapa with bountiful compassion, endless energy, and an unswerving will to fight the government. His commitment inspired many

(opposite page) KALAUPAPA VILLAGE, far down dizzying cliffs, is easily seen from the mule/hiking trail which begins near Palaau State Park.

others to help the settlement become more liveable, adding hospitals, stores, cars, gardens — even beer and ice cream. In 1941, when sulfone drugs were found to arrest Hansen's Disease (leprosy's official euphemism) — hope settled over the colony at last.

Since 1980, the entire peninsula, three adjacent valleys (Waialeia, Waihanau, Waikolu), a huge wedge of sea cliffs and mountain rain forest, as well as 2,000 acres of shoreline, ocean, and offshore islands, have come under the protective jurisdiction of the U.S. National Park Service as Kalaupapa National Historical Park.

The Park Service renovates historical sites, poisons noxious plants, helps to preserve native ecosystems, constructs pig-proof fences to improve the watershed, controls goats in efforts to arrest soil erosion, and brings a new level of security to its dwindling residents.

Kalaupapa embraced a wealth of *yin* and *yang*: barren, lush; plains, cliffs; dry, wet; hot, cold; windy, calm; love, hate; heaven, hell. Here man's most animalistic nature co-existed with overwhelming altruism, and brute territoriality dominated over passivity until curbed by care from Damien and those who followed.

In a real sense, the dreaded disease had dehumanized a total society, not just the early lepers. In a frantic effort to save the healthy, the diseased were tossed into an environment where Nature's laws, not man's, ruled. The government acted out of the terror that everyone in Hawaii might perish. What was incalculably harsh for the lepers was widely accepted as necessary by society as a whole, as for over sixty years foreign diseases had already decimated the native Hawaiian populace.

Today, several tour companies offer personalized guided tours of the settlement and peninsula. Although it is impossible to contract leprosy here now, current law prohibits children under 16 years. As Kalaupapa is also a restricted area, tour reservations should be made in advance and/or permission obtained from Hawaii's Department of Health. If these rules are not followed, you may land at the airport and find yourself sitting alone within five minutes — no planes, no taxis, no check-in desk, and no one to "sponsor" you! Remember to bring plenty of color film and anything else you might need; there are no stores, restaurants, public drinking fountains, or other amenities.

A neatly tended garden frames FATHER DAMIEN'S MONUMENT.

PALAAU STATE PARK

No trip to Molokai is complete without a trip to PALAAU STATE PARK. For most visitors, this is their sole land-based view of Kalaupapa Peninsula and the majestic sea cliffs of the north coast. Though windy, it is one of the few spots on Molokai where camping is permitted. There is no charge and the time limit is seven days. To locate the park, about twenty minutes' drive from the airport, head three miles east on Route 46, then turn left on Route 47. Pass Kualapuu — home of the Del Monte Pineapple Company for fifty years — and climb through forest, past an arboretum, to the highway's end.

(below) The famous (infamous?) PHALLIC ROCK, reached by a short trail, stands erect amidst a grove of feathery ironwood trees. Six feet high, these realistic stone genitals — admittedly carved a little over the years — are purported to emanate powers corresponding to their shape, thus serving as a traditional pilgrimage site for barren women. Because Molokai is an island of mysterious happenings, we do not recommend lone women to visit Kauleonanahoa ("Nanahoa's penis") after dark, no matter how curious they may be.

(top) Bathed in effulgent light, the formidable CLIFFS which isolate Kalaupapa from "topside" (the rest of Molokai) are seen from the trail *(center)* and central peninsula.

(bottom right) HOOFPRINTS in the *pali* (cliff) trail zigzag steadily downward through dry, windswept scrub. Although each hoofprint is deeply embedded in the trail (this photo was taken in 1981), as of 1989, not one mule nor rider has yet fallen over the cliffs!

(bottom left) Almost impenetrable forest and dissected valleys lie close to the *pali*.

Molokai Mule Ride/PIC

(above & below left) Molokai's renowned MULE RIDE is guaranteed to raise your adrenaline level. Scaling the face of a 1,600-foot precipice, from close to Palaau State Park down to Kalaupapa Peninsula, is an indescribable, intensely personal experience. Seasoned hikers who do not balk at a 3,200-foot elevation change in one day, may prefer "shank's pony." If neither riding nor hiking sounds appealing, a short walk from Palaau State Park parking lot culminates in a stunning view similar to this photo. Hikers and riders please note: previous permission is required to descend to the peninsula; a mandatory fee covers lunch and guided tour. Contact Damien Molokai Tours, P.O. Box 1, Kalaupapa, HI 96742, 808-567-6171 or Molokai Mule Ride, P.O. Box 200, Kualapuu, HI 96757, 808-567-6088. Visiting Kalaupapa is like visiting Russia in the old days — you could not "do it on your own"!

(above) Lovely AWAHUA BEACH, skirting the base of the *"pali"* marks the beginning of another unforgettable adventure, the peninsula tour, which includes lunch and beverages.

KALAUPAPA SETTLEMENT

This neat, colorful, crime-free village is unique. Its hundred residents, mostly patients ranging from their 50s to 90s, are gentle people with admirable inner strength. Their afflictions are noncontagious and since the 1940s, sulfone drugs have been used to arrest the disease. Interestingly, small numbers of people (primarily Vietnamese) immigrating to Honolulu have Hansen's Disease. None have been sent to Kalaupapa. Thanks to modern medicine, all are now treated as outpatients.

Patients are well cared for and live a relatively normal life but most, due to old age and poor eyesight, are sedentary, spending most of their time watching TV or talking on the phone. Richard Marks, one of the youngest and earliest to receive treatment, is exceptionally energetic. Social life is limited to the bar, church, library, or potluck party. There is a Visitor Center with bookstore here.

Gone are the days when patients were gawked at like caged animals. Modern times have spawned a respect that is unique in leper history. These people remind us — silently, movingly — that we all belong to the global family. Their close community is a truly Hawaiian *ohana* (extended family). For some, Kalaupapa has been their sole home for more than forty years. Since 1969 all have been free to leave; those that remain do so by choice. Thirty years ago, a resident would face six months imprisonment for playing hookie — now a few patients have even visited Las Vegas, Europe, and China!

(above) A colorful GAS STATION caters to a limited driving clientele. If supplies run low, mules may come to the rescue — not to ride, but to haul gasoline from "topside"! Everyone has two or three cars and an equal number of televisions, as repairs generally take months.

(top) The OLD HOSPITAL was built in 1932. Inside is a screen which formerly separated patients and visitors. Nearby, a modern treatment center is administered by the State Department of Health.

(center) Twice a year, barges from Honolulu deliver supplies to KALAUPAPA'S DOCK. Airplanes deal with emergencies, but understandably, services and commodities are limited. In order to protect the privacy of the residents, the entire county of Kalawao is off-limits to the public; private yachts may anchor only with previous written permission.

(bottom) Date palms and other INTRODUCED PLANTS clothe Waialeia Gulch; upslope, introduced mammals create such environmental disturbance that the watersheds harbor some of the worst pollution in Hawaii. The National Park Service has installed an expensive new water system in Kalawao derived entirely from spring water, thus reducing health hazards to Kalaupapa's residents. Hopefully the Park's management efforts will increasingly protect the dwindling native ecosystems within Kalawao County.

Parking on grass, small planes bring visitors to the minuscule AIRPORT, here highlighted by brooding storm clouds. Behind sits the "Molokai Light," Hawaii's largest and brightest beacon until recently, when a modern searchlight replaced its antiquated lens, imported from France around 1900.

Although State law mandates that leprosy be officially termed Hansen's Disease, after the Norwegian who discovered the bacillus in 1873, residents at Kalaupapa feel more comfortable with the old terminology.* On meeting and spending time with them (most of whom have lived on the peninsula all their lives and were eager to pose for photos), one perceives strength of character and a surprising lightheartedness. Over half no longer require daily medications.

Apart from the medical advances, Hawaii has made tremendous social contributions toward educating the world about leprosy. Outdated laws are disappearing, although not as fast as residents wish. Big breakthroughs include peninsular tours, and patients' freedom to travel and to entertain visitors. Rules pertaining to permission and minors, however, still exist.

*Following the patients' lead and the internationally known history of Kalaupapa, we continue to use the words "leper" and "leprosy" in this book. It does not imply uncleanness or forced segregation.

Distant Siloama Church.

(center right) Seen from closer to the settlement, Molokai's Wester Cliffs recede into the horizontal.

(bottom right) The OUTSKIRTS OF TOWN. Horses and cattle, previously allowed to roam freely, have recently been removed to protect native plants and prevent the spread of noxious weeds.

(opposite page) Dawn's translucent light bathes a lonely corner of Kalaupapa Peninsula , whose relatively recent volcanic origin is betrayed by smooth black expanses of PAHOEHOE LAVA. Kauhako Crater, from which lava flowed, lies just *mauka* (toward the mountain) of the lighthouse.

(above) Peering through a window of ST. PHILOMENA'S CHURCH at Kalawao, one can see the graveyard where Father Damien was buried. Beyond lies the precipitous north shore.

Faith in God was imperative to survival in Kalaupapa's isolated outposts. Even today churches are vital to the community. First established was the Protestant SILOAMA CHURCH, "Church of the Healing Spring" (1866), often dwarfed by a misty backdrop. The present church, third on the site, was most recently renovated in 1966.

110

(above) ST. PHILOMENA'S CHURCH, assembled in Honolulu in 1872 and transported to Kalaupapa, is sometimes referred to as "Father Damien's Church." It was here that the revered priest installed cuplike spittoons in the floor so that lepers with congested lungs could attend services indoors.

(below) Immediately behind Siloama Church, a rubbly pasture leads to the TORTURED LAVA SHORE. Rumors claim that fearful crewmen literally kicked "the unclean" into this bay.

(top) After close to 1,000 years of habitation, Kalaupapa is one of the state's richest archaeological preserves — this is another reason for its inclusion in the U.S. National Park system. Exciting new finds include this LARGE CEMETERY, recently unearthed near Puu Uao.

(center & bottom left) The dark recesses of WAIHANAU GULCH, seen from the crater lookout, lead into dense rain forests covering deeply dissected country contorted in humps and vales like huge egg cartons.

(bottom right) Rows of GRAVES glimmer in the failing light at St. Philomena's. A mile offshore, appropriately bathed in effulgence, looms a sanctuary for new life, Mokapu Island Seabird Sanctuary (pron. "mow-kah-poo"). To locals, it is Pan Dulce, "Portuguese Sweet Bread Island" because of its shape.

As recently as 8,000 years ago — a mere second of geological time — a tiny volcanic crater popped up from the ocean floor midway along Molokai's northern coast. Its resultant lava flows created Kalaupapa Peninsula roughly as it is seen today, a shallow shield volcano sloping imperceptibly into a flat, tongue-shaped plain. Its 405-foot-high dome, PUU UAO LOOKOUT (pron. "pu-u u-ow," rhymes with "moo cow"), the site of a long-established burial site, affords expansive views in every direction. About 8,000 people lived (and died) at Kalaupapa, primarily from 1866 to 1945.

(center) KAUHAKO CRATER, visible from Puu Uao Lookout, is claimed by limnologists to be one of the most peculiar lakes in the world. Its deep columnar tube, layered with fresh, brackish, and salt water, and extending 400 feet below sea level, is home to two species of native shrimp. Remnant dryland forests, uncommon elsewhere, cling to its rubbly walls. They harbor rare plants such as *wauke*, from which bark cloth (*tapa*) was made, and IHI (*Portulaca sclerocarpa*), a diminutive succulent *(bottom)*. Legend credits the digging of this crater to Pele, Hawaii's goddess of fire, who, after striking water here, proceeded to work her flaming transformations on the island of Maui.

(top) FATHER DAMIEN'S ORIGINAL GRAVESTONE is at St. Philomena's Church; his bones now lie in Belgium. For sixteen years this noble priest, whose name has become synonymous with Kalaupapa, was doctor, nurse, confessor, mayor, coffin-builder, funeral director, choir-master, and jack-of-all-trades until he, too, succumbed to the dreaded disease. In 1977, the Roman Catholic Church bestowed upon him the title Venerable Father Damien, a step on the road to sainthood. Brother Dutton and Mother Marianne were also notable figures in Kalaupapa's history, instilling truly humane values into the patients for forty-four and thirty-five years, respectively.

(bottom right) KENSO SEPI, a jovial Kalaupapa resident, carves coconut bowls in his tiny workshop. He is also the inventor of innovative aids to help his companions button shirts and open flip-top cans.

(below) Prior to 1969, strict segregation laws prohibited the mingling of patients and non-patients. Even the BATHROOMS had two "sexes": patients and *kokua* (helpers).

(top) IVY KAHILIHIWA
KUUPOLILAUAEOMA-KANA *(right)*,
whose tongue-twisting but descrip-
tive Hawaiian name means "I give to
you my bosom" or "the island of
Kauai," works at the library. *(center)*
KENSO SEPI, an artisan, cuts
HERBERT HAYASE'S hair on a sunny
afternoon. With hair now trimmed,
HERBERT HAYASE smiles handsomely
(bottom right).

(bottom left) MARIANO RUX tends
the sole bar on Molokai's north
shore. As of 1988, 4,000 cases of beer
passed annually through his modest
establishment.

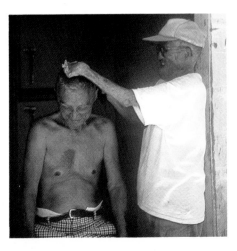

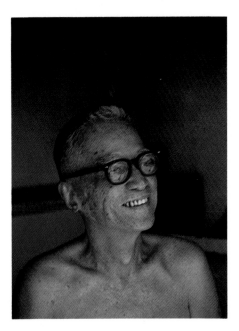

(above) Swathed in glorious radiance, tiny KALAWAO, dating from 1866, (pron. "kah-lah-wow") was Kalaupapa's original settlement site. Its population peaked at 1,174 in 1890. Long a ghost town, Kalawao is slowly undergoing renovation by the Park Service. Both Siloama and St. Philomena are found here, a long, bumpy ride from Kalaupapa township. Keep your eyes peeled for green turtles as you admire this bay from the Kalawao Park lookout.

(center) For many early lepers, this MAGNIFICENT VIEW was their last. Impaired vision and blindness were among leprosy's symptoms. The eyes of many residents today are still weak from the days before sulfone and other drugs. The ladies, especially, wear hats to protect their eyes from the sun.

(bottom) A lone *hala* tree and stone wall weather a heavy downpour. Offshore, in WAIALEIA BAY, early lepers struggled to stay afloat in turbulent seas laced with jagged lava. Survivors were dumped — bruised and penniless — onto wavetossed boulders.

(right) A shallow SHELTER CAVE. In the early days, this was an enviable shelter, just as seen here. It was difficult for lepers to lift stones, as their fingers, in advanced cases of the disease, were mere stubs.

(below) This coveted LAVA-TUBE CAVE, providing the only natural roof on the peninsula, was inhabited until relatively recently, according to Richard Marks, owner and guide for Damien Molokai Tours and a pioneer in public education about Kalaupapa. He is seen here chatting with one of the authors. As a teenager, Marks spent a few years as a runaway seaman before coming to Kalaupapa in 1950.

(top) This TAHITIAN-STYLE MARAE (pron. "mah-rye," a place of worship) is an unusual construction in Hawaii.

(center) BIRTHING STONES (*pohaku hanau*) are revered artifacts; few still exist. These ancient "maternity beds" were believed to emanate spiritual strength (*mana*) during labor and birth. After medical care arrived in Kalaupapa, newborns were immediately whisked away to Honolulu. For years, mothers still preferred the refuge of this birthing stone, not only for its good luck, but for precious moments of cuddling before their infants were taken away forever.

(bottom) HOUSE-SITE on the eastern shore. Throughout Hawaii, walled house-sites such as this are assumed to have had roofs. Not here. Prior to Father Damien's arrival, lepers owned little more than a crudely constructed windbreak, rags, and deteriorating bodies. They ate what they could find or catch. There was no medicine until 1905, when the U.S. Congress appropriated $100,000 for a hospital and laboratory at Kalaupapa: it unfortunately was short-lived.

For decades, grossly insufficient food and supplies were sent to Kalaupapa. This MILLION-DOLLAR VIEW is from the underground lava tube which, despite its jagged interior and dampness, at least provided shelter, *opihi* (limpets), *limu* (seaweed), and occasionally fish.

(below) Kalaupapa was an ideal NATURAL PRISON, guaranteed to isolate its unfortunate inmates. Its barren tongue (8,500 acres), surrounded by rough seas and jagged lavas, was subject to gnarly storms, baking heat, and constant winds. For a full 360 degrees, formidable topographic barriers greeted the eye. A geological afterthought stuck onto unscaleable cliffs, Kalaupapa was completely severed from the rest of Molokai: there was no escape. Three tantalizing valleys — Waihanau (center), Waialeia (upper left), and Waikolu (further left), — were undoubtedly explored. Even if the cliffs were climbed, topside "egg carton" topography, blind ridges, vertical rock faces, dizzying waterfalls, serpentine watercourses, abundant fog, and almost impenetrable vegetation would certainly have drained every shred of energy from hopeful runaways. Without map and compass, even modern woodsmen would be hard pressed to reach Kaunakakai.

(center) Adjacent to the coastal cliffs, carpets of tiny NATIVE DAISIES (*Tetromolopium luteiodiscus*) were recently described as a new species endemic to Molokai. This wee gem has miraculously survived decades of grazing, but its numbers are few.

The establishment of Kalaupapa National Historical Park in 1980 brought many positive changes. Park Service officials renovated historical sites, poisoned noxious plants, constructed pig-proof fences to preserve remnant native eco-systems, improved the watershed, controlled goats to arrest soil erosion, and brought a new level of security to its dwindling population. Weeds like LANTANA (*Lantana camara*), **top right**, were cleared, while the best carpets of HINAHINA (*Heliotropum anomalum*) in Hawaii, **(below)**, were protected. It is appropriate that *hinahina*, named after Hina, goddess of the moon, should still grow in abundance on Molokai, since legend relates that Molokai is the daughter of the moon.

(bottom right) Purple Thunbergias creep over walls, perhaps unique in human history — laid with severely crippled hands.

(above) FINGERS OF LAVA penetrate the deep blue ocean, while a sudden turn in the weather stirs calm waters into crashing waves, geyser-like spumes and SALTY CASCADES, *(below)*.

These GLOWING CLOUDS are momentarily serene, yet how quickly a change of mood occurs.

North coast moods shift with the fleeting whimsy of clouds. Light rain highlights a remarkable TRIO OF ISLANDS that are to this day unexplored by biologists. From left to right, Huelo, Okala, and Mokapu dot the silvery sea in front of Kalaupapa Peninsula. Seabirds including frigates, petrels, shearwaters, tropicbirds, and noddy terns frequent these cliffs and seas. TORRENTIAL DOWNPOURS practically obliterate Molokai's north shore. Ancient Hawaiians accepted rain as a gift from the gods. The following ancient chant seems appropriate for this scene, with Kalaupapa, once a distressingly sad place, in the distance:

> Loving is the water which
> moistens the edge of the cloud,
> It is welling over in tears,
> Weeping at the beach until out of breath;
> Weeping from the beach to the uplands to be quieted.

CHAPTER VI INTERIOR MOUNTAINS

THIS FINAL CHAPTER takes us to the wildest, wettest, most isolated part of the island. It is a lavish green land beyond roads, off the beaten track, once the domain of the powerful ancient god, Ku. Few see its interior, although the accessible fringes awe visitors with unsuspected beauty. Far above the sea, it is dominated by mist and rain, biting winds, stunted plants, and dense forests. Unique plants, snails, birds, and entire ecosystems lie sequestered within its vertical palisades, deep gorges, and isolated plateaus. This hidden wilderness is considered so valuable that in the 1980s three separate government agencies created four contiguous reserves to protect its treasures. It is worthy of national park status.

This land crowns the eastern mountaintops, lying above 2,500-foot elevation, beginning where the clouds cling to the mountain on a normal day. It can be seen from Kaunakakai, barely five miles away from Kalaupapa (Chapter V), from the South Shore (Chapter II), and along its northern flanks from Palaau State Park. It is deeply notched by the great northern valleys of the North Shore (Chapter IV), ending abruptly at their mighty sea cliffs, all of which are visible from commercial airplanes.

Were it not for a single, unmarked dirt road, its expanses would be limited to hunters and adventurous hikers. However, a Forest Reserve jeep road (no rental cars please; four-wheel drives are available) exits Highway 46 about halfway between the airport and Kaunakakai, just east of a concrete bridge and about a half-mile south of Route 47 (Kualapuu Road). This dusty, bumpy track climbs steadily past pineapple fields and the large red hill, Puu Luahine (go left when a road bears right toward it). It winds upward, past dry fields, scattered trees, a Nature Conservancy camp, eucalyptus forests, and narrow ridges covered with ferns, becoming increasingly wet until at last it eases alongside Waikolu Valley, offering one of the most breathtaking spectacles in Hawaii. The Waikolu Picnic Grove at the lookout provides camping, picnic tables, and restrooms. Beyond lies a maze of jeep roads (mostly dead ends) and trails, accessible to hardy hikers only through The Nature Conservancy and the Dept. of Land and Natural Resources.

One of the twin "KAHUNA'S TEARS" WATERFALLS, over 1,000 feet high, is the lifeblood of Molokai.

(top) TWIN FALLS, "Kahuna's Tears," epitomize the magnificent wild scenery encountered en route to WAIKOLU VALLEY LOOKOUT. Their waters, captured below, are diverted through a seven-mile tunnel to help fill the 1.4 billion gallon reservoir at Kualapuu, Molokai's major source of water.

(center) The sinuous course of WAIHANAU STREAM, clothed in native forests, typifies the highly dissected nature of Molokai's uplands.

(bottom left) In an oft-repeated scene, a pig-dog seizes his struggling prey in a DRAMATIC BATTLE. If the hunter arrives too late, the dog could be killed. Molokai hunters are very adept at capturing pigs from accessible forests. More than half a mile from a road or trail, however, pig numbers increase dramatically. On the U.S. mainland, remote areas are best left alone; in Hawaii the opposite is true. Unless the terrain is vertical or surrounded by cliffs impassable to feral mammals *(bottom right)*, the land must be actively managed with fences and control efforts if forests are to survive.

Pete Barrett / DLNR

This incredible view of part of Kalaupapa National Historic Park, from HANALI-LOLILO TRAIL, is reached by a ten-minute hike from the Waikolu Valley Lookout.

PRISTINE HAWAII: virgin rain forest of incredible beauty crowns isolated Olokui Plateau, a prehistoric jewel in the State of Hawaii's Natural Reserve System.

Clothing Molokai's highest mountain lies wilderness of such value that a national panel of ecologists recommended including it in a nationwide system of "unique ecosystems." When the government was unable to act, The Nature Conservancy of Hawaii (TNCH) acquired perpetual management rights from the landowner, Molokai Ranch, Ltd., over 2,774 acres of this forested watershed, naming it KAMAKOU PRESERVE. Pig fences, hunting programs, and the control of alien plants are helping to restore the natural conditions; this in turn improves the quality and quantity of water. Road and trail repairs have improved recreation opportunities. Endangered birds, such as the extremely rare Molokai Thrush have a better chance of survival. Immediately to the north of the preserve, the State of Hawaii has established the Puu Alii Natural Area Reserve, a 1,330-acre area managed jointly with the National Park Service and The Nature Conservancy.

Often rivers find old lava tubes and race underground to the bewilderment of hikers, who may wander into a canyon with no apparent outlet. The Nature Conservancy offers pre-planned, guided hikes into the reserve or write to the Kamakou Preserve Manager, Box 40, Kuakapuu, HI 96757, including a stamped, self-addressed envelope. Hikers must be fit — this is not easy strolling!

Kamakou Preserve embraces a variety of habitats and is home to approximately 250 kinds of native plants, 219 of which are endemic to Hawaii. Its leeward edges receive less rainfall than the ridgetops, and thus support a drier forest. Trees such as the abundant OHIA, *Metrosideros collina **(all three photos)** — once so sacred that commoners were severely punished for touching it or even standing in its shadow — shrink to shrubbiness or rise in grandeur, depending on rainfall.

(above) In yet another guise, the *ohia* in upland bogs are severely dwarfed. This tiny mature OHIA "TREE" is not much taller than its own flower! The soggy, acidic soils are so deficient in oxygen and nitrogen that only a few finely adapted plants can survive.

(below) PEPEOPAE BOG (pron. "pay-pay-oh-pie"), a remarkable island of life hidden within Kamakou's wet forest, is traversed by a boardwalk on Hanalilolilo Trail. Allow three hours for the round trip from the Waikolu Valley overlook.

The Nature conservancy-Hawaii

There are only a few areas in the Hawaiian archipelago that are so inaccessible that they have been able to survive the major changes of the past two centuries. The largest is Olokui Plateau, now protected by the State of Hawaii as a Natural Area Reserve. It owes its isolation to an impregnable bastion of cliffs 3,000 to 4,000 feet high. Its pristine forests have never known the rooting of pigs nor the browsing of goats and deer. Spanning 1,620 acres of deeply dissected terrain, this living quilt buffers the assaults of drenching rains and high winds, enabling tender orchids and a myriad other delicate forms of life to thrive in rare abundance. The same geological forces which shaped valleys, isolated people, and contributed to the remarkable evolution of

birds, plants, and land snails even more varied than those described by Darwin in the Galapagos Islands, have preserved a fragment of Hawaii's ancient past.

(below) A FERNY VISTA beckons the eye. Although scarcely a mile away, the misty ridge beyond is inaccessible. One can reach Olokui's exiled world only by dangling from a swaying helicopter cable, and then only with written permission. This is fitting since an international resource is best protected as a scientific treasure trove, an exclusive gauge of how Hawaii, and other similar environments, used to be.

An outstanding pristine forest, a rarity in Hawaii, where introduced mammals are almost ubiquitous.

(above) So green and entangled is Olokui that all traces of the soil disappear beneath the LACY VERDURE. In a gulch like this, the tinkling sounds beneath interlacing fern fronds once warned us of a sixty-foot drop to a streambed completely entombed in the ferny dusk.

(top right) As a drenching, three-day storm abates, sparkling rays of sun dissipate the cloudy abyss along Olokui's western rim, HAPAPA PALI.

(right) Although appearing flat from a distance, Olokui's highly dissected plateau, like most of Molokai's interior mountains, is extraordinarily difficult to traverse. An UNNAMED WATERFALL flows through hauntingly beautiful greenery. Water droplets forever unite land and sea in a glorious panorama of clouds, streams, waterfalls, and lush vegetation.

133

(right) Hawaii's showy begonia, the *puamakanui* (*Hillebrandia sandwicensis*), may grow to a height of five feet. The shoots of both these native plants entice pigs just as catnip lures cats.

(center) Restricted entirely to a small acreage around 4,000 feet, this LOBELIA TREE (*Clermontia sp.*), unknown to science before 1980, is a new addition to the catalog of Hawaii's natural wealth.

(below) Huge floral wheels of KOLII (*Trematolobelia macrostachys*), their spokes ablaze with cerise flowers, spotlight Olokui's forest by the thousands. This close-up of *kolii's* curved blossoms highlights one of Hawaii's showiest native plants. It occurs statewide but nowhere in such profusion.

One of Molokai's special LOBELIA flowers (*Cyanea pallida*), several inches long, is found only on steep slopes and in pristine forests.

(top) IEIE (*Freycinetia arborea*), a spirally vine, was once dedicated to the forest god, Ku. Ancient Polynesian seers perceived the basic unity of life and energy — for example, *ieie* was considered a link between land and sea, earth and sky, natural and supernatural.

(center & below) Pale FOREST VIOLETS, *Viola chamissoniana* (=*V. robusta*), atop woody stems a foot high, are Kamakou specialties. Seven species of violets grace the Hawaiian Islands, where they inhabit saturated soils in forests and bogs, generally above 2,000 feet elevation. Most species are found on the older islands. Thus Kauai holds four species (two found only there), Oahu has three, while Maui and Molokai share two species each. Only a single species is found on the Big Island, where it is restricted to the older Kohala Mountains. Hawaiian violets may surprise you; unlike their North American relatives: some species produce woody stems more than two feet tall!

Bob Gustafson

Bob Gustafson

Wind-whipped ELFIN WOODLAND atop Olokui Peak (4,602 feet), rarely touched by the sun, glows with an aura of timeless purity.

John Carothers

Clothed in camouflaged colors, Hawaii's NATIVE ORCHIDS — all inconspicuous mountain dwellers — are disappointing. To the layperson they recall Cinderella before the fairy godmother arrived.

Water-loving "lower plants" — MOSSES, LIVERWORTS, FILMY FERNS — crowd, collage-like, on a tree fern trunk.

Hawaii's extraordinarily diverse native birds are a classic study in evolution, even more striking than the famed Darwin's finches of the Galapagos Islands. Their original 120-odd species range from a few inches to three feet high and include a number of flightless forms. One subfamily, the Drepanidinae, includes birds that resemble warblers, parrots, woodpeckers, honeyeaters, and huge-billed finches. Over eighty percent of Hawaii's birds are either extinct or endangered, figures not exceeded anywhere else in the world. Much of this loss is due to a Mexican mosquito, introduced in 1828, which transmits fatal diseases to native birds. Tough birds, such as mynahs and doves, are unaffected. Molokai's approximate 5,000-foot height makes most of its forests favorable to mosquitos, thus only the hardiest native birds can survive. Fossils from Moomomi and the annals of early naturalists reveal a far richer diversity of birds than today's prime forests hold. Trails within Kamakou Preserve provide the best venue for observing those that still remain.

Introduced birds that inhabit Molokai's lowlands as well as its interior forests — doves and white-eyes among them — are pictured in chapter one.

Robert Western

The APAPANE (*Himatione sanguinea*), Hawaii's most abundant native bird, is unmistakable with its glossy black wings and deep red body. It is seen above 3,000-feet elevation among ohia flowers, where its constant twittering adds an aural dimension to island forests.

The ravages of leprosy found a counterpart among Hawaii's birds. *(above & right)* An Apapane lies dead and scarred from AVIAN POX, introduced to the islands by a flourishing cage-bird trade 100 years ago.

Howard Hunt

Handsomely attired in orange, yellow, red and gray, the RED-BILLED LEIOTHRIX (*Leiothrix lutea*) was brought to Hawaii from China in 1911. On Molokai it frequents dense vegetation above 3,000 feet, where it weaves a deep, cup-shaped NEST and lays two to four blue eggs.

(Upper) This poignant painting by Cheryl Boynton, depicting an AVIAN GRAVEYARD, relates the catastrophic losses of Hawaii's native birds during the last 1,500 years. Unfortunately, nothing can be done about those that succumb to mosquito-borne diseases, but essential habitats can be preserved to enhance the survival rate of those that remain.

(center) Appareled in cryptic brown, the MOLOKAI THRUSH or *olomao* (*Myadestes lanaiensis*) is designed to evade enemies and competitors as it seeks berries and insects. Eyeless enemies — viruses living in mosquitos — have, however, wrought war on this thrush, once common on Molokai, Maui, and Lanai, reducing its numbers to less than fifty individuals worldwide. Their principal refuges are Kamakou Preserve and Olokui Natural Area Reserve. Those familiar with robins or wood thrushes can imagine how the sweet, liquid song of the Molokai thrush must have enriched the natural sounds of Molokai's original forests.

Douglas Pratt

(bottom) The dazzling vermilion plumage and orange bill of the splendid IIWI (*Vestiaria coccinea*) (pron. "ee-ee-vee"), who spend most of their time sipping flower nectar and gleaning foliage insects, is now rarely sighted on Molokai — scarcely 100 birds cling to a tenuous existence along the highest ridges of the great northern valleys.

Robert Western

THE SANDALWOOD TRADE

Hawaii's sandalwood was discovered accidentally in 1790 when a ship's captain cooked dinner over firewood purchased on Kauai. Already the world's known sandalwood resources were fast disappearing, and it was a popular trading item. While it lasted, in the early nineteenth century, Hawaii's sandalwood was a bonanza to canny traders, who brought an estimated $4 million worth of unnecessary luxuries and alcohol into Hawaii, thus creating an enormous debt to be paid with the precious wood. Hawaiian chiefs forced their subjects into hard labor to collect the booty; this resulted in much hardship, a decline in island self-sufficiency, a breakdown of a traditional Polynesian society, and irreparable damage to Hawaii's forests. Molokai was essentially stripped to the roots of its last sandalwood; only the odd individual tree still survives on the steep backwalls of the great northern valleys.

For millenia, SANDALWOOD has been coveted and ruthlessly exploited. The aromatic oils of its heartwood exude a captivating odor for fifty years after the wood is cut. For centuries it has been used for incense, cosmetics, perfumes, massage lubricants, household ornaments, and religious items.

En route to Waikolu Valley is an authentic SANDALWOOD PIT (*lua moku ili-ahi*), a hold-sized template for sandalwood loads. When filled with logs, its "cargo" would be carried on native backs to a waiting vessel. Many malnourished Hawaiians perished en route.

(bottom right) The four-petalled Flowers of an uncommon Maui sandalwood (*Santalum haleakalae*), an epitaph to this lamentable chapter of Hawaiian history.

INDEX

ABOUT THE AUTHORS

Cameron and Kay Kepler met in Honolulu in 1964 while Kay was an East-West Center foreign student, and Cameron was studying Pacific seabirds for the U.S. National Museum. They have worked together as a biological team since their marriage in Honolulu in 1966. Kay, a naturalized New Zealander, was born in Australia, while Cameron hails from California. Both successfully pursued Ph.D. degrees in vertebrate zoology at Cornell University, New York, Kay receiving degrees en route from the University of Canterbury, New Zealand, and the University of Hawaii, Honolulu, while Cam completed degrees at the University of California, Santa Barbara. Over the past two decades they have authored or co-authored twelve books, over sixty scientific publications, and numerous technical reports. Kay has also written articles on biological aspects of the Hawaiian Islands. Cam is an endangered species field biologist with the U.S. Fish and Wildlife Service. Together the Keplers have conducted forest bird and plant surveys, seabird studies, and endangered species research worldwide specializing in Hawaii and the Pacific.

INSIDE BACK COVER: An eloquent moment of stillness captured from Keawanui Cave, northeast Molokai. Photo: James Maragos.

FRONT COVER: Molokai's famous mule ride. Photo Douglas Peebles.

BACK COVER: Golden dusk at Kupuaiwa Grove highlights the timeless Polynesian tranquility that still endures on Molokai. Photo Robert Abraham.